Align

GET YOUR TEAM ON THE SAME PAGE

DISCOVER CLIENTS' NEEDS

DEVELOP BETTER PRODUCTS

LAURA REESE

ixia
PRESS

Mineola, New York

Bibliographical Note

Align: Get Your Team on the Same Page, Discover Clients' Needs, Develop Better Products is a new work, first published by Ixia Press in 2019.

Library of Congress Cataloging-in-Publication Data

Names: Reese, Laura Marie, author.
Title: Align : get your team on the same page, discover clients' needs,
  develop better products / Laura Marie Reese.
Description: Mineola, New York : Ixia Press, 2019.
Identifiers: LCCN 2018021717| ISBN 9780486816456 (hardback) |
  ISBN 0486816451
Subjects: LCSH: Customer relations. | Consumer satisfaction. | BISAC:
  BUSINESS & ECONOMICS / Customer Relations. | BUSINESS &
  ECONOMICS / Management Science.
Classification: LCC HF5415.5 .R4354 2019 | DDC 658.8/12—dc23
LC record available at https://lccn.loc.gov/2018021717

Ixia Press
An imprint of Dover Publications, Inc.

Manufactured in the United States by LSC Communications
81645101   2019
www.doverpublications.com/ixiapress

This book is dedicated to all those who would rather wing it when meeting with customers.
To you, I say, "Read this book."

Contents

Preface

THIS BOOK is based on my experiences directing the customer advisory board (CAB) program at Altera Corporation for more than a decade. Our company designed computer chips that went into various products, from Internet networking routers to high-end medical equipment. Quite independent of our specific products, the protocol we came up with for working with customers via the CAB program could work for any business-to-business (B2B) industry. It would be wise to set up procedures such as those we developed for any B2B company serious about setting long-range strategy. Getting information about challenges faced by your clients directly from the source will allow your team to anticipate client needs in a way that is true to reality.

It all started when my boss at the time, Robert Blake, complained that we seemed to be planning products by looking in the rearview mirror. He wanted us to stop looking backward and start peering into the future.

We agreed on our purpose straightaway: to align our product road maps with our key customers. We wasted no time and invited these customers to meet face-to-face with us at our headquarters in San Jose, California. In these forums, we strove to learn about their product road maps, with an eye toward developing goods they would want to buy in the future.

Understanding what customers want is neither an easy nor an obvious task. You can't simply throw a few customers and product planners in a room and say, "Go!" There's more to it than simply asking, "Hey, what do you want us to build for you?" At least, that's what we came to learn after a few initial rocky meetings.

What we learned—the hard way—was this: Engaging directly with customers can be fraught with pitfalls. Unintended expectations can be set, sore topics mentioned, or one might alienate the customers by talking too much, pitching unwanted products, or failing to listen. As it turns out, simply throwing a group of people in a room and seeing what shakes loose is a recipe for disaster. Even if those people have developed best-in-class skills as subject matter experts (SMEs in tech parlance), they might not be bringing to the table a terribly competent interpersonal game. Even if the SMEs are socially adept, if they come into the room unclear of their purpose or untrained in the techniques of uncovering customer needs, they could unintentionally scuttle the meeting.

Regarding SMEs: usually this term applies to specialized engineers, but I'll use it throughout the book to denote anyone with a highly focused knowledge base, whether it be in corporate accounting, patent protection, web marketing, or your own bailiwick.

I've witnessed bright and highly valued SMEs face-plant fantastically in meetings. They attempted to uncover customer needs but hadn't been given any guidance. They weren't to be blamed; they put their energy and focus into their specialties, not into customer-facing skills. So I shared with them simple, easy-to-remember techniques that made it effortless to interact with customers and hear insights that mattered, which they could use in developing products. I explained the various roles of each person on the aligning team, so the SMEs could know the right moments to contribute to the conversation.

Aligning with customers face-to-face is worth doing. To do it well requires planning, training, and focus. During my decade of running the customer advisory board program, my colleagues and I learned many lessons. I also gleaned knowledge from books and mentors. I've included these insights here. My hope is that by sharing my experience, I can give you a jump start into uncovering customer needs successfully.

This book is for all people in businesses who want to understand their customers. It's geared toward supplier-to-manufacturer or B2B relationships more than, say, the relationship between a high-volume consumer goods manufacturer and its customers. That said, many of these techniques could translate to businesses where there is a lot of interaction directly with individual end customers.

In this book you'll find:

- ways to cultivate an aligning mind-set;

- clear roles for each member of the uncovering team;

- step-by-step guides for running customer alignment meetings;

- specific skills for face-to-face engagement with customers;

- example scenarios inspired by real experiences; and

- tips for putting it all together.

Derived from concepts and skills that proved to be effective for us in the customer advisory board program, these ideas transformed us from a disparate group of individual amateurs to a team of professionals. I hope they can do the same for you.

Acknowledgments

I'D LIKE TO THANK Robert Blake and Paul Ekas—Paul, for suggesting I write this book, and Robert, for asking me to put together something called a customer advisory board (CAB) program way back when. Both encouraged my work bringing product developers together with key customers to align our respective companies' road maps.

I'd also like to thank Rob Sturgill, Andy Turudic, Mike Hutton, and Dirk Reese (my husband), who kindly allowed me to interview them about their experiences being subject matter experts (SMEs) in customer meetings. Eva Condron has my gratitude for providing insightful feedback on many occasions.

Credit goes to Rory Clark for introducing me to active listening techniques, among other skills in his Focus Selling training. Bill Brown and Elena Meyers, both superbly skillful salespeople, provided feedback for my CAB program. George Papa, vice president of sales, supported the meetings by encouraging his teams to bring important customers in to talk with us "factory" folks.

Sean Atsatt recommended many books to consult, and Martin Lee provided insightful tips for interacting directly with customers. People from the engineering department, including John Costello and Richard Cliff, deserve thanks for attending so many meetings and demonstrating how to listen and strive for genuine understanding.

Thanks to Andy Turudic for providing feedback on the manuscript during various revisions.

Also, I thank all the people who follow me on the Mr. Money Mustache forum. They offered feedback on beta drafts and encouraged me to keep writing.

Last, I thank my parents not only for molding me into who I have become but also for giving me the opportunity to pursue an engineering degree at a top university. That education led directly to my career at Altera Corporation (now a part of Intel Corporation). I thank Altera Corporation for allowing me the space in which to develop the CAB program, which sparked the experiences and insights that led to writing this book.

The concepts, examples, and strategies are my own, or derived from associates with whom I've worked, or gleaned from books and courses. However, the advice herein in no way represents any officially endorsed processes or procedures of Altera Corporation.

People are referred to by their full names. In some examples, fictitious names are used, and any similarities to real people are coincidental and unintended.

CHAPTER ONE

The Power of Preparation

"Give me six hours to chop down a tree, and I will spend the first four sharpening the axe." —Abraham Lincoln

ARRIVING AT WORK one morning, I was in an upbeat mood. A strategic customer alignment (CA) meeting with a customer was scheduled for ten o'clock. Everyone was ready, and every detail had been taken care of.

An e-mail marked "Urgent" greeted me. It was from Nathan. I had a bad feeling about it. Nathan was my key attendee, our linchpin subject matter expert. As I opened the e-mail, I prayed, "Please don't cancel. Please don't let me down."

Unfortunately, my fears were confirmed. "Laura, I'm sorry. I can't attend the meeting today. There's an accident on Highway 17. Besides, I'm fighting a nasty head cold. I recommend Sarah as my replacement—she's on cc. If she can't make it, call me at home and I'll help you find an alternate. Nathan."

How disappointing. This client, whom we'll call Ginormo Corporation, was one of our company's largest customers. GC accounted for more than 10 percent of our revenue. The particular division that would be joining us in only an hour's time drove a healthy chunk of that business. They were industry leaders. Therefore, we were eager to align our product road map of Field Programmable Gate Arrays (FPGAs) with them. (Think customizable logic computer chip.)

We'd heard nothing but radio silence from GC for months, but now they were sending four valuable employees to meet with us: an in-the-trenches engineer, two influential engineering directors, and the chief technology officer. Their strong lineup was hardly an expression of love for us, however. Rather, it was testimony to the fact that our products were critical to their success. The truth was they weren't our biggest fans at that moment. We'd burned them recently with a software update, which, for various reasons, had set their schedule back by weeks, maybe months. The market they served was intensely competitive. Time to market meant everything, and that update had compromised their plans. No, they were not happy with us.

Thankfully, the software issue had been resolved just in time for this meeting. However, wounds were still fresh. It wouldn't be easy to get them to open up, and that was one reason why I needed Nathan. He was great with customers. If anyone could unlock customer information, it was he. For one thing, he brought technical credibility, and nothing keeps engineers talking than an audience that enthusiastically comprehends what they're saying. But there was more to it than mere understanding. When you get engineers around a whiteboard, discussing a problem, you see camaraderie, ad hoc teaming, exploration, creativity, brainstorming, common purpose, head scratching, and inspiration. There's something special about a conversation between people who share an in-depth understanding of a complex topic. Nathan was the kind of colleague who could connect in this manner with just about anyone, no matter their personality type. His knowledge of our products and of the industry as a whole was simultaneously broad and deep. Yep, Nathan was perfect. But Nathan wouldn't be coming.

I should have been in a panic, but I was calm. How could that be?

Short answer: because we'd prepared. We'd developed and carefully implemented an aligning protocol, so I was confident I could draw on a team of competent attendees. Nathan's alternate would bring all the technical credibility that was required. More important, I was confident she would ask skillful questions, build trust with the customer, and demonstrate genuine interest. She'd connect, and in the end, she'd strengthen relationships. How did I know? Because I'd taught her how.

Rewind a few years, however, and the prospect of inviting an alternate to a customer meeting would have been as appealing to me as a round of Russian roulette. Back then, there were only a handful of people whom I felt comfortable putting in front of customers. Even those colleagues could be unpredictable. But an unfamiliar alternate? No way. They might talk too much or ask leading questions. Worst of all, they might attempt to sell the customers on our products, coming off like a sleazy used-car salesperson. I'd seen every cringe-worthy behavior you could imagine.

To be fair, colleagues from engineering, marketing, and other departments usually behaved professionally. It was simply glaringly notable the few times when they goofed. The problem was that I never knew when they were going to derail the conversation. Even the most diplomatic among them, including high-level executives, could make awkward comments or steer the discussion off course. Whether due to outrageous gaffes or peccadilloes, each misstep added up over the course of a meeting. The consequences were consistent: the customer would stop talking, and we'd come away with little useful information.

So why did we continue? Why did we keep hosting meetings? Because sometimes magic happened—we'd connect. Everyone could feel it. The conversation would carry forward on its own as excitement built. Suddenly, the customer would jump up, grab a dry erase marker, and brainstorm ideas on the whiteboard. Thus inspired, we were in flow. Pencils scratched over engineering notepads, and laptop keys clicked. We happily recorded outpourings of customer insights, ideas, and visions.

Out of that magic came revelations that we might never have encountered. A deep understanding emerged of what the customer was truly trying to do and why. We learned what was getting in their way and explored how we might help them overcome such obstacles. We heard stories, not just data points. We understood the context, relative importance, and reasons for each request.

On these occasions, I'd wonder, could we cultivate that magic regularly and consistently? Could we avoid whatever prevented that magic from materializing?

I began observing our behavior in the margins of my notes. After a few customer meetings, the truth emerged: we were winging it.

People were coming to the meetings unprepared. They had skipped premeetings and hadn't read e-mail briefings. They'd show up and steer the conversation according to their own agendas. Otherwise cordial colleagues became argumentative when they didn't hear answers they wanted to hear. I wondered, didn't people know how to behave?

Then I imagined myself in my colleagues' shoes. Like me, they had decisions to make, projects to push forward, and interminable meetings to endure. These meetings took them away from their work. They wanted to make the most of their time, so they'd rapid-fire all their open questions at each customer, whether the topics were relevant or not. It wasn't pretty.

But I was as much to blame as they were. I was dumping them into an impossible position. They were expected to behave well with customers, but I hadn't clarified what specific behaviors were expected. I hadn't confirmed their understanding of the meeting goals, nor whether they knew their specific roles in the meetings. I hadn't provided behavioral tips, such as how to ask skillful questions or how to take useful notes. No, I hadn't set expectations and yet I expected perfect behavior. How naive.

So I took action. First, I educated myself. I sought guidance and found wisdom in books and trainings. I learned how to question and actively listen to customers, using techniques taught by Rory Clark, the creator of Focus $elling. His program trained salespeople to diagnose customer situations prior to prescribing solutions. I borrowed many of his techniques, especially those rooted in active listening, and taught them to my colleagues.

As I developed the training program, I also received valuable feedback from a colleague in the human resources department, the ever insightful Eva Condron, who is currently the senior manager of global talent development at Xilinx, Inc. (our archrival!).

I was eager and ready to go. I developed a training class and invited about fifteen people. Two people showed up. I let the others know that if they wanted to meet with customers, they were required to undergo training. I petitioned the heads of each department to nudge their teams to attend. In the end, nearly everyone I asked took this training. What I found was that while reluctant at first, most of them embraced what they learned. They felt relieved because they finally understood, with absolute clarity, what their roles and responsibilities were. They were gratified to learn exactly what was expected of them and, more important, what was *not* expected. They developed customer aligning skills and contributed their own ideas for improving customer engagements. I happily incorporated their insights into subsequent training sessions.

Within a year, our meetings had transformed. We spent less time preparing and more time gathering useful information. With success came demand from the sales organization. The field teams had long been wary of putting their customers in front of what they called "loose cannon factory people." With visibility and positive customer chatter about our meetings, the sales teams became more comfortable with bringing customers to us. They increasingly saw these meetings as a means of strengthening relationships with their accounts. For example, the vice president of sales, George Papa, began hearing positive reviews from customers. Recognizing the relationship-building power of these meetings, he encouraged his sales teams to arrange more of them. Before long, we had more requests than we could reasonably schedule.

People naturally formed personal connections with customers in these meetings. Over time, they felt comfortable sending one-off e-mails to close customers to ask their take on new technologies or experiences with current products. When I moved on to a new role, planning "stacked 3-D" products, I was able to tap into a wide network of valuable opinions that helped me form a good understanding of how this technology would best serve our customers. These insights would have been hidden from me if I hadn't attended so many customer alignment meetings.

Attendees from our engineering teams also found value. Whereas in the past, they were reluctant to accept invitations, at some point their attitudes switched and they began requesting invitations. Previously, these meetings were regarded as disruptions to their schedules and a source of annoying action items. After attending the training, they saw value in hearing directly from customers. They came to understand that the objective was not to pick up action items, but to learn customer goals and challenges in an open forum. I witnessed a total transformation. Formerly mute and defensive engineers began asking questions from a place of genuine curiosity. Rather than wringing their hands over their own constraints, they actively strove to learn what the customer was trying to accomplish and why.

As for me? Well, our planning documents transformed. What previously were little more than lists of customer requirements became stories of how various features would be valued by various customers. Second, I gained confidence in what we'd come to call ourselves: the "uncovering team." Dozens of colleagues, across multiple departments, could be called upon at any time to help us in the product planning department to uncover information we needed in order to define products that aligned with customer plans. We became a unit, capable of working together to uncover customer information that mattered.

And so we found ourselves in a good place by the time Ginormo Corp was due to visit. And we'd be fine, even without a key subject matter expert.

As I replied to Nathan's e-mail, I was calm and relaxed. Sarah would be up to the task. She'd bring all the technical credibility we needed. More important, I was confident she would ask skillful questions, build trust with the customer, and demonstrate genuine interest. She'd connect and strengthen our relationships.

You see, learning customer goals and challenges and aligning with customers can be a vital part of determining internal strategy. Gaining reliable knowledge in customer alignment meetings requires planning. Each attendee must be trained to use his or her innate skills in the context of a larger team effort. All players must understand their role within the team and play that role at the right time. This doesn't mean people must alter their personalities. They simply need to adjust some wording when they ask questions, take proper notes, and sharpen their listening skills. All this can be learned, and all this can be taught, as proven through the training protocol I developed.

While this training was developed in the context of the semiconductor industry and many examples derive from that world, the concepts translate to industries outside of Silicon Valley. If your goal is to align with customers or stakeholders in any field, this book will help show the way. These concepts can work for nonprofit organizations, accounting agencies, widget manufacturers, or law offices. The guidance contained herein is a starting point. Use what works for you, adjust the advice as it makes sense for your situation, and build upon your experience.

These techniques are not complicated. Anyone can learn them, including technical engineers, experienced marketers, and even high-level executives.

BUT I WANT TO WING IT!

You may think you're a great communicator and don't need external guidance. Maybe you even think that when you wing it, you outperform your hyperprepared colleagues. You're more natural, relatable, at ease. That may be so, but for us it was clear that winging it in our customer alignment meetings wasn't working. While I, too, like thinking on my feet, and in many cases find planning and training to be annoying, I realized that by failing to develop our customer interfacing skills, we spent too many mental cycles thinking about what to say. Worse yet, for those of us who spent no time thinking about what to say, the results could be disastrous. Feet were inserted into mouths regularly.

Corporations usually provide sales training to their customer-facing employees but don't extend such lessons to their internal engineering and planning personnel. When subject matter experts lack basic training, however, sales teams loathe when they show up to customer meetings. They're unknown quantities and could derail the relationship with one half-baked comment. That's unfortunate because, often, customer insights that matter most are aired precisely when customers talk directly with those creating a company's services, not only those tasked with selling them.

This book bridges that gap. It provides easy-to-remember tips for reliably interacting with customers. The goal isn't about issue resolution here, but rather about aligning road maps and improving the planning process by eliciting trustworthy, unbiased, and useful customer insights and information. This kind of customer-facing training is essential. Subject matter experts can be key to working with customers, most especially so when they have the skills to interact with tact and precision.

Ask yourself this: What's your focus during a customer meeting? Is it on questioning techniques? Interpersonal skills? Probably not. No, you focus on the content of the discussion and, as you do, you naturally snap into whatever conversational habits you've developed over your life. That could mean you interrupt as soon as you disagree with what's being said. Or it could be you ask verbose and wandering questions that do more telling than asking. In some contexts, these tendencies have merit. In others, they are disruptive. Conversely, going by instinct could mean you never utter a peep. Silence could result in failing to gain critical information too.

To lay the ground for a useful discussion, conversational skills must be molded into habit, so you don't have to think about them. In other words, the way we question and listen needs to be automatic or second nature, so we are free to focus on the content of the conversation.

Once you've learned how to align with your customers, you may be motivated to bring others onboard.

Still with me? Still not sold? Don't worry, I've anticipated this reaction and will help you overcome it. Below you'll find common objections I've heard from colleagues who wanted to opt out of training, who were opposed to change. Underneath each objection, I've written my typical responses. Sometimes I convinced the heretics with these arguments. Other times, I convinced their bosses to "convince" them. Read them all with an open mind, and I hope I will convince you too.

"I'm already great with people. I can opt out of training. Right?"

Uh, no. Even if you're a hit at parties, you need alignment skills training. Here's why.

Effective customer alignment meetings are team efforts that require specific planning and specialized language. Imagine a professional soccer match (football, if you are outside of the United States). Each player knows his or her role and what part of the field to cover while the ball is being handled elsewhere. Now imagine a soccer game of six-year-olds. Every player rushes for the ball wherever it is. They run over one another, trip up, and in the end, the ball moves haphazardly. This vision of young children playing soccer came to mind often in those days prior to training, as colleagues bumbled across the conversational field. Which team do you want to play on? Winning with professionals or losing with a bunch of novices?

When you're part of a team, you know your role. You know when to step back and let your teammates carry the ball. You identify when your teammate is in trouble and assist without getting in the way. Teammates with common training can execute strategies and pivot to new tactics as needed. They think as one.

Second, even if you're good with people, you may find that training improves your game. Those benefits can extend beyond the customer meeting conference room. When I learned these skills, I was raising two elementary-school-age daughters. I used my newfound skills at home and discovered they invited independent thinking and honest communication. My oldest daughter used to argue with me on seemingly everything. When I learned to suppress unintended messaging, she seemed to argue less. For example, I might say that I'm exhausted dealing with finding her stuff all over the place. She'd argue that we leave stuff all over too. Using these methods, I learned to think about what I really wanted to communicate. I began forming requests such as "Please put your coat where it belongs." It was tough for her to argue with that. Also, she didn't feel a need to because she wasn't being personally attacked.

Before I learned these skills, my younger daughter seemed reluctant to tell me about what was going on at school. After I learned how to ask open-ended questions that focused on *her* reality, not mine, she began sharing—a lot. Eventually, I learned that a girl, whom I'd thought was her best friend, was, in fact, bullying her.

Both daughters began cooperating with me, mainly because I began communicating with them skillfully. I engaged with them genuinely, not with manipulative comments or crude systems of punishment and rewards. The use of communication techniques embedded in customer aligning enabled my daughters and me to talk to each other as partners working toward common solutions, rather than as adversaries. That's how it should be in customer meetings as well.

The benefit to our home life was a pleasant byproduct. In the end, if you're unwilling to learn the common language of aligning and how to work with your team, it is probably best that you don't attend customer alignment meetings. At best, you'd be a fifth wheel. At worst, you'd disrupt the game. But I'd encourage you to be teachable and make the choice to collaborate in discovering information that matters along with the whole team.

"I'm too busy. I don't have time for this stuff."

If you're invited to customer meetings and the people organizing the meetings have recommended you learn these communication techniques, there's a reason. Learning these skills will save you time in the long run. You'll learn a common language for aligning. When everyone is working from the same playbook, preparation meetings take less time because everyone on the team immediately grasps his or her own roles and goals. When everyone on the team knows common aligning tactics and skills, it frees you to focus on the particulars of each customer. You may find that customer meetings become more efficient and enjoyable, since you now avoid wasting time on conversations that offer little value.

Note that this goes for executives too. When everyone has a team strategy, but the vice president of some department has no idea what it is, the plans can go awry very quickly, sometimes leading to an entire meeting being wasted or damaging a relationship.

"I'm an expert in my field. The last thing I need is more corporate training."

If you're a key attendee and are frequently consulted as an expert in your subject area, there's a chance you've cultivated a bit of a rock star status. Your work is critical to operations, and everybody knows it. That's awesome. Congratulations. People respect your work.

You've probably put a lot of toil into your subject of expertise. Now I invite you to put a small amount of time and effort into honing your interpersonal aligning skills so that you can play the role in a customer alignment meeting that you are uniquely qualified to play. By pulling lessons from this book, you'll understand what the rest of the team is doing and can sit back as you let the team position the customer to a place where you may begin hearing insights from a fresh perspective on your topic. Perhaps the discussion will illuminate how the customer uses your products in unexpected ways. Revelations about how your technology might be improved, streamlined, or altered may come to mind. Knowing how your work is being deployed by users may give you new insights and improve your work, allowing your output to continue improving. As true masters know, a key to success is to always be learning. The skills taught in this book will power-boost the insights you'll glean from customers.

"I'm an introvert. I'm terrible at talking with people. The last thing I want to do is meet with customers."

Fair enough. Perhaps all this talk of connecting with customers is scaring you off. Don't worry. There are ways of managing customer meetings so that you can talk sparingly. In fact, your reticence to open your mouth is likely an asset. This is because the goal is not for the customer to listen to *you*, but for you to listen to *the customer*. The majority of the talking should be done by the customer, which means the majority of the *listening* will be done by *you*. That said, by learning the concepts contained in this book, you may identify times when your voice is needed in the conversation. The skills you learn here can help you find your most effective voice.

Preparation and training may lessen anxiety over speaking, and enhance your value in the workplace by making you more visible in other contexts as you grow comfortable chiming in. You may find yourself engaging helpfully and confidently in conversation, especially when the topic moves on to material familiar only to you. Give it a chance and, with practice, you'll find this both becomes easier and enhances your ability to navigate both personal and professional situations far beyond customer alignment meetings.

Yes, every customer alignment meeting attendee must undergo training.

Whether you burst with confidence or lack it entirely, it takes but one untrained person to completely derail a meeting. It doesn't matter if you're an introvert or an extrovert, a preening rock star or a silent wallflower. If you go into a customer meeting winging it or failing to play a specific role on the team, you could unwittingly do real damage. You don't want to be that person. Do you?

Once you and your team stop getting in the way of gathering information that matters, your path to growth may open up. What's your company trying to achieve? Are you trying to create the best product within your market? To explore new niches? To continually improve customer satisfaction? To gain and retain more clients? All the above?

If you want to be a valued contributor to moving the company forward, then I'd advise you to do everything you can to align your company with key customers. Getting their feedback and using it to chart your company's strategic course will enhance your edge against competitors and set you on track to accomplish your strategic goals. This communication training in customer alignment is your ticket to do just that.

CHAPTER TWO

Roles and Responsibilities

"To me, teamwork is the beauty of our sport, where you have five acting as one. You become selfless."
—Mike Krzyzewski, Duke University men's basketball coach

Each attendee in a customer alignment meeting has specific responsibilities and roles to play. As with an effective basketball team, you can't have everyone posting up under the hoop. You need a point guard at the top of the key too.

It used to be that players were assigned positions and that was it. When Mike Krzyzewski coached the US national men's basketball team, however, he famously implemented a positionless team. What this meant was that each player had the skills and knowledge to play any position at any time. They were interchangeable. Though unorthodox, it worked wonders. His teams won gold in Beijing, London, and Rio de Janeiro.

Similarly, in customer alignment meetings, attendees must be aware of all roles and which role they're playing that day. If everyone is capable of filling in all roles as needed, the team will be more effective overall. Throughout this book, we'll call this team that acts as one the "uncovering team" or "aligning team," because you'll be working together uncovering customer goals and aligning product road maps as real professionals.

To reinforce this edict, I'm going to repeat it another way: learn every role, not just the one you expect to play most often, and soon you'll be performing like champions, discovering customer information that matters most and, in time, building better products.

In this chapter, we're going to jump right into the precise roles and responsibilities of each team member. We're starting with the nuts and bolts. Later, we'll discuss the more philosophical mind-sets critical to each role.

First, let's start by talking about a member of the team who never switches. I'm taking about the life of the party, the source of our livelihoods, that most esteemed attendee: the customer.

CUSTOMER

In my industry, we tend to invite system architects, chief technical officers, computer chip designers, board designers, and product planners from customer companies. The titles in your industry may differ. The point is to invite people who not only understand their company's long-term strategy but also are shaping it.

At least a week before the meeting, the customer should be briefed as to what to expect. They should prepare a presentation about their situation. They'll present toward the beginning of the meeting. The customer's responsibility is to share their plans, goals, challenges, and view of the world.

The customer's role is that of adviser. Not an adviser for what your company should develop but an adviser in giving insight into the goals and challenges they are facing. Their role is to convey that information fully so that your company can take it and use it to inform your planning activities as it makes the most sense, given your core competency and goals.

Invite Professors, Not Gilligans

Many people follow the path of least resistance and invite whomever they happen to personally know at the customer company. Or they blindly invite people based on titles. Bad move! Here's why.

The 1960s TV show *Gilligan's Island* featured a daffy dolt named Gilligan. Nobody listened to him. He had zero impact on the decisions the group of castaways made. Conversely, the Professor was seen by everyone as a source of wisdom and insight. His opinion heavily influenced the group.

Imagine a company filled with lots of Gilligans and a few Professors. Who among them do you think you should invite to a customer alignment meeting? That's right, the Professors.

That makes sense, of course. Yet, when left to their own planning, people tend to invite Gilligans. I suspect it is because Gilligans are easy to find and more willing to accept invitations. Gilligans can be found along the path of least resistance. They may be people we already know. What's easier than inviting a friend to a meeting? But the easy way isn't always the right way. Before inviting your acquaintances, make sure they are Professors.

That's not to say Gilligans are stupid or worthless. Often, they have solid understandings of some topics. The problem is they have little influence within their organization. Why should you listen to someone whose company doesn't listen to them? As my colleague Rob Sturgill noted, "It's important to remember that one person does not necessarily represent the views of everyone in a customer company. In the first meeting, you might meet with a person of little influence or insight [a Gilligan]. He says almost nothing useful but then elaborates on market plans. Later, after taking these market plans as gospel, your team might discover totally contrary info and direction from the CEO and chief architect."

Also, Gilligans tend not to see the big picture. You want to align with people who understand where their company fits in the market, where their company is going, and why. You don't want Gilligan for this; you want the Professor.

A Professor is a person of vision. She has insight into her market and exerts influence within her organization. You can even invite two Professors. One could be an influential planning director and the other, a nuts-and-bolts, in-the-trenches engineer. Both should have the full confidence of their leadership.

Finding the Professor isn't as simple as looking at an organizational chart and seeking out a lofty title. You've got to dig deeper. For example, the organizational chart might lead you to invite the senior vice president of engineering. But what if that person is a waffling doofus? The senior vice president may have a big title but zero influence. Perhaps one hand is on a golden-parachute rip cord. No one seeks this senior vice president's counsel anymore, so why should you? Invite this senior vice president to a customer alignment meeting and you'll collect marginally useful information. While you're wasting your time with the senior vice president, you're missing out on the person you need to talk to. This might be a director who reports to the CTO. That director may be the most influential and market-savvy employee in the entire company. That's who you want to invite.

Rarely does an attendee possess all these attributes. That's why we tended to invite two or three people from the customer company. Together, they had all the knowledge, insight, responsibility, and influence needed to contribute to a successful meeting. Seeing them hash out their plans among themselves could be very instructive.

Find the thought leaders at target companies. Often, these people have an element of humility to them. They might qualify their opinions with "I could be wrong . . ." or "Others might have different assessments. . . ." They're the kind of people who are comfortable understanding and discussing various solutions without getting married to one in particular. They may have strong views, but they tend not to be dogmatic, as they converse at length about benefits that various solutions might offer.

Work with the sales team to identify who the right people may be, making sure you aren't just reaching for your own chums.

Meet with One Customer Division at a Time

Customer alignment meetings are best when held with one customer division at a time. This means that if Company XYZ is a conglomerate composed of eight divisions that build eight different products, it's best to hold eight separate sessions. Meet with one division at a time and discuss one product at a time. If you host a meeting with people from multiple product groups, you'll have a hard time making sense of the conversation, much less your notes after the fact. Goals and challenges of various departments may clash with one another. It's hard enough to understand one customer's perspective. Three at once is a mess. Avoid this by holding separate customer alignment meetings for each customer division.

One Customer Company at a Time

Avoid inviting people from different customer companies. If you invite people from Company B along with people from Company C, you may find no one speaks candidly. Even if they're not direct competitors, they may feel uncomfortable divulging information to people who, in their opinion, have no good reason for being there.

What If the Customer Sends a Substitute?

On occasion, the Professor says she can't make it and sends in her place a Gilligan. If it's too late to cancel, you might need to suck it up and have the meeting. If the meeting is still a long way off, I'd suggest you reschedule to a time when the Professor can attend. Let her know that your team is eager to meet with her specifically. Explain that you are keen to make sure your team has a full understanding of her company's goals and challenges, and you would very much like to hear it from her.

HOSTS

The most effective host, in my experience, is a personable person who understands both the customer's market and the technical aspects of the products under discussion. They tend to be senior managers from our product planning department or strategic marketing engineers from our business units. Sometimes, account managers make effective hosts as well. The important thing is for the host to have one foot in marketing and one foot in technical product knowledge. Well, not only that. They must also be somewhat personable and comfortable leading a meeting.

The host's top responsibility is to look after the comfort of the customers in attendance. He'll write the agenda on a board or easel in the conference room. He'll kick off the meeting, lead introductions, and call breaks. He'll decide whether to stick to the agenda or whether to let a conversation go on.

The host runs the premeeting and is responsible for making sure all presenters, subject matter experts, and scribes (notetakers) know what's expected of them. The host is responsible for setting expectations with the customers in advance of the customer alignment meeting and making sure they prepare.

The host is ultimately responsible for making sure all notes from all scribes are received within one business day of the customer alignment meeting. The host is also responsible for running the follow-up meeting and making sure final notes are published both to the customers and internally, to all stakeholders.

Oftentimes, the host is also the meeting organizer. But it doesn't have to be that way. It's up to you. If you have a lot of available employees, break up these roles, because it can be a lot for one person to manage. That will free up the host to focus on meeting content, skills, notes, and follow-up, without being distracted by meeting setup logistics.

The host is the team leader whose roles and responsibilities are to . . .

- prepare the customer for the meeting;
- ensure customer comfort during the CA meeting;
- manage conversation so all stakeholders get what they need;
- ensure team member roles and responsibilities are understood;
- lead the team in uncovering customer goals and challenges; and
- make sure notes are posted and distributed adequately.

MEETING ORGANIZERS

The meeting organizer is the chief tactical officer of the customer alignment meeting. He is responsible for booking the premeeting, the meeting, and the postmeeting. The job entails ensuring that all meeting logistics are arranged, such as conference room reservations, catering, gifts, badges, and any security clearances.

The meeting organizer checks head count issues and works with the host to manage them. He ensures the conference room is set up with adequate seating and proper materials such as easel, whiteboard, and projector.

If one person is host and a different person is the meeting organizer, the roles must be clearly defined. If it makes better sense for the host to book meetings and for the meeting organizer to publish the notes internally, then so be it. No matter who handles what, make sure that all the responsibilities are taken care of.

The meeting organizer is the master of logistics. His role is to . . .

- ensure conference room and catering are adequate;
- set up meeting to promote customer comfort (travel, badges, Wi-Fi, etc.);
- book premeetings, customer alignment sessions, and postmeetings;
- make sure reference material is online and accessible to stakeholders; and
- assign roles to every attendee, including notetakers.

PRESENTER

A presenter's role is to lead the discussion during a specific session. The objective is both to share information about plans and to prompt customers to share more about their specific goals and challenges.

Customer alignment meetings are not for selling. Sales pitches are not appropriate here. Presenters need to be mindful of what they are presenting because the goal is not to educate the customer, but to encourage feedback and further discussion to learn what customers are trying to do.

Presentations should be focused on the future. They should present possible products and ideas, for example, whatever the company road map is. But be careful. You do not want to come off as if you are telling the customer how things are going to be. Anything presented should be done so with the intent of getting feedback and direction.

Be clear that the plans you present could change in the future. Make sure to set expectations appropriately. On one hand, you don't want to raise hopes that you're going to solve every problem. But, on the other, you want to foster a discussion that allows you to ask pointed trade-off questions and get honest replies.

The paramount responsibility of the presenter is to customize the discussion so that it matches with the customer's interests. Every presenter should attend the customer's presentation of their goals and challenges. During that session, the presenter should note what topics are relevant to the customer and which are not. The presenter can further refine questions they want to ask.

SALES

These are the roles and responsibilities of the sales team.

Brief the entire aligning team.

Salespeople take a lead role in preparing the uncovering team for the customer alignment meeting. It's their responsibility to explain who the customers are. They share what they know to be the customer temperaments, their interests, and any history—good or bad—that the customer has experienced with the company. They review the customer's relationship with competitors, as well as their place within their own market.

If the customer is known for having an aggressive legal team who claims joint inventions after meeting with their suppliers, make sure everyone in the meeting is aware of this fact. They will need to take care to withhold proprietary information and limit the discussion to strictly learning what the customers are trying to do. I am not a lawyer, so I will not give specific legal advice, but I will advise that you consult with your legal team. That said, this kind of button-lip situation is rare in my experience. Regardless, it's the sales team's responsibility to make sure legal considerations are understood by everyone on the uncovering team.

To sum up, the sales team's main role is to share any and all relevant information they are aware of, especially about customers attending customer alignment meetings for the first time. Ideally, the sales team shares this information during the premeeting.

Monitor customer; adjust course if needed.

In the customer alignment meeting itself, the sales team is to monitor the customer's comfort level. If they detect discomfort, then they need to assess whether to take action. Sometimes, discomfort is constructive. For example, the customer might be challenged to think about an engineering problem in a new way and is deep in thought. This discomfort is good and should be allowed to proceed unobstructed. Other times, however, people on the uncovering team might go beyond challenging an idea and the customer may interpret their comments as hostile. In the moment, people can get excited and forget their training. Hey, it happens. It's up to the sales team to keep watch. If they think the customer is being treated unfairly or see that the customer is shutting down for any reason at all, then it's up to the customer advocate (the sales rep) to ask for a break and work with the host to get the meeting back on track.

Of course, the uncovering team should not be treating customers as hostile witnesses. They should continue asking questions that conform to the techniques explained, starting from Chapter Seven "Aligning Skills: Questioning." That said, you want someone to take action if people get carried away in the discussion and unwittingly upset the customer. This is a primary responsibility of the salesperson.

Record action items.

Anyone who signs up for an action item is expected to note what they signed up for and follow up on it after the meeting, without being prompted. That said, it's in the sales team's interest to hold these people to account. During the customer alignment meeting, the sales team should record all action items that are taken. After the meeting, they are responsible for sending these action items to the host, so they can be collated into the meeting notes. A few days after the meeting, the sales team can nudge people who volunteered for action.

Note: in a customer alignment meeting, action items are to be avoided unless they're absolutely necessary. This meeting is about learning customer objectives. The purpose is not to close current-issue action items. That said, if any one group is responsible for making sure all action items are followed up on, it's the sales team. Why? Because the sales team cares the most about the customer relationship. Ideally, you, if you're part of the sales team, won't have to lift a finger because everyone who attends the meeting understands that it is their responsibility to follow up on their own actions. That said, you'd be wise to follow up.

EXECUTIVES

Members of the senior executive staff may be experts on some topic that the customer will be discussing, or they may be invited simply to convey that your company is genuinely interested in hearing what the customer has to say. If you are an executive, please know that you are first and foremost filling the role of subject matter expert. Therefore, please familiarize yourself with the responsibilities of an SME.

Briefly convey your stature but, more important, your interest.

During the introductions, share your title as well as your interest in the customer. Express sincerely how their time and partnership are valued by you and the wider team. Do keep your comments brief.

When the customer starts their presentation, become an equal member of the uncovering team. Learn the skills described in the upcoming chapters of this book, just like the rest of the team. Remember Mike Krzyzewski's position-less basketball team. Develop the skills and knowledge to play any position at any time, knowing that for most of the game, you'll fill the role of subject matter expert.

For example, on occasion, restate what you heard the customer say. Use the customer's own phrasing. This will project powerful signals to everyone in the room. It will tell the customer that you're listening and genuinely striving to understand the situation they're facing. It also will remind the team of your shared goal: uncovering information that matters.

Listen.

Whether in the meeting for ten minutes or two hours, you will primarily listen. Participate with the team using open-ended, customer-centric, and future-oriented questions. Ask these questions from a place of genuine interest in understanding the customer's situation.

Let customers answer for themselves.

Your teammates may ask questions that seem foolish. Even if your first inclination is to bail out the customer by answering on their behalf, don't. *Let the customer answer.* Get comfortable with silence and wait. Remember, you want to give customers the freedom to answer in their own way. "Rescuing" customers by answering on their behalf might bias them toward answers you want to hear. This goes against the very purpose for hosting customer alignment meetings: to hear what the customer is trying to do, *in their own words.*

NOTETAKERS AKA SCRIBES

If you are tasked with taking notes as a meeting scribe, you are expected to know what portion of the meeting you're responsible for recording, to know what subject you're to pay special attention to, and to take verbatim notes.

If you are tasked with taking notes, you are expected to do the following:

- Take verbatim notes—exactly what the customer says, using the customer's own words and colloquialisms.

- Write down the questions asked by your teammates, if the answers make better sense with the questions. (Usually, the answers can stand alone.)

- Record action items, clearly marked so they can be spotted quickly when scanning the notes.

- If you are a *topic scribe*, record all customer comments that fall within a particular topic.

- If you are a *session scribe*, record all customer comments during your designated session.

Type up, clean up, and submit your notes within *one day* of the meeting.

If you feel you cannot physically take notes for the duration of the session you've been assigned, then work with the host to adjust. Consider taking turns with other notetakers in order to spread out the work. This is a grueling job, and it's the most important job. Make sure you don't sign up for more than you can handle. Letting information slip away without being recorded can lead to the team failing to truly learn the full customer story. Take this job seriously and make sure notes are taken during every session.

If no one seems to be taking notes, simply ask who has been assigned the task for the session. The team should be able to come up with an answer on the spot.

SUBJECT MATTER EXPERTS (SMEs)

I've saved the most critical role for last. Subject matter experts (SMEs) make or break customer alignment meetings. SMEs are knowledgeable on topics that the customer and your company want to discuss. SMEs bring technical credibility to the conversation. They are often the reason the customer took time out to meet with you.

Often, people will have multiple roles, many times including that of SME.

Not only do SMEs demonstrate credibility with customers, they can be uniquely adept at understanding what the customers are saying. They are uniquely qualified to ask probing questions that get at what customers are trying to do and then follow up with further questions that uncover more meaningful information.

SMEs must understand their roles within the meeting. First and foremost, their role is to listen and learn the customer's goals and challenges. Yes, their goal is the same as everyone else's. But they are uniquely qualified to do this.

SMEs are well positioned to cultivate engineer-to-engineer partnership. You want customers to know they're being heard by the people who are designing the products they'll be using. An SME does exactly that when listening with an open mind and when they ask questions from a genuine place of curiosity. Also, when SMEs go back to their desks, they then take with them a real understanding of how customers use the products they build. They can recall the customer's perspective at any time when making decisions on product design, big or small.

Bear in mind that this power comes with grave danger. If an SME only attends one customer alignment meeting, that SME risks generalizing one customer's perspective as being representative of all customers. This can put up blinders. So, please, anyone attending customer alignment meetings as an SME should plan to attend many.

Every single SME should know his or her role and should have been trained in alignment skills. An SME who knows how to interact with customers, using the questioning techniques explained in subsequent chapters, can play a key role in unlocking customer goals and challenges. Furthermore, SMEs can ensure the entire team translates these needs to real product requirements with fidelity.

SMEs are critical for understanding customer stories. Without SMEs, the implied requirements of a customer's goals or challenges may be oversimplified or distorted by someone not well versed in the topic at hand. SMEs are needed to make sure the technical bits are understood by the team.

If you have been invited to a customer alignment meeting as an SME, here are your specific roles and responsibilities:

- Strive to genuinely understand the customer's goals and challenges by asking open-ended, customer-centric, and future-oriented questions. Support the lines of questioning initiated by others on your team, even if outside your area of expertise.

- Demonstrate credibility but take care not to talk too much. The point of the meeting is to learn the customer's goals and challenges, not to hear you drone on about your accomplishments. Look to the host for guidance.

- If there's enough time, take this opportunity to identify how the customer uses your company's products, especially the portion you're responsible for. But do not lead with this line of questioning as it's coming from a selfish perspective.

- Learn what's important to the customer and why.

- Ask confirmation questions that only you, with expertise in that field, can ask.

- Record verbatim notes, especially those comments that have to do with your particular area of interest and expertise.

That's what's expected of SMEs in customer alignment meetings.

What Not to Do in a Customer Alignment Meeting

The following are a few things you absolutely should not do. By the way, they may seem obvious, but these are specific behaviors

I have personally observed untrained SMEs demonstrating, so let's be clear:

- Don't interpret customer requests as action items. Instead, ask what's motivating their request.

- Don't tell customers that their requests are absurd. Instead, ask what's motivating their request.

- Don't tell customers how difficult it would be to implement their requests. Instead, ask what's motivating their request.

- Don't use the meeting as a forum for listing your accomplishments or to parade your ego.

- Don't tell customers they don't know what they're talking about. Instead, ask them where they got the evidence for their opinion or what's motivating their suggestions.

- Don't talk too much; instead, listen more.

- Don't educate customers about what you think they should know, unless you have this discussion well after you've uncovered their full story. Then you can point out topics they might want to read up on.

That's a lot of don'ts, and maybe they seem obvious. However, I've seen many SMEs, at one time or another, do all the above no-nos. Be aware of these and steer clear. As you can see, the alternative is usually to get curious and inquire as to what's behind the statements they've made. In chapters four and five about goals and mind-sets, we'll discuss these alternatives further.

CHAPTER THREE

Customer Alignment Meetings

"You've got to start with the customer experience and work back toward the technology—not the other way around."
—Steve Jobs

WHY ALIGN AND HOW?

STEVE JOBS famously said, "It's really hard to design products by focus groups. A lot of times, people don't know what they want until you show it to them."

I can't tell you how many times I've heard colleagues, especially from the marketing department, repeat some variation of this quote. Sometimes, they were deflecting a disconfirming data point that we'd gathered from a customer. Or they were claiming that meeting with customers held little value.

Whoa! How does one combat the sentiments of a Silicon Valley deity such as Jobs?

All I could do was agree. Maybe that sounds crazy, since this book is about aligning with customers. But parse the statement out. "A lot of times, people don't know what they want until you show it to them." In other words, they can't tell you what they want until they imagine what's possible. Indeed, an important part of a customer alignment meeting is to explicitly share what your company is capable of delivering. But you don't lead with what's possible. First, you uncover their story.

The timing and order of discussion matter. After over a decade in these kinds of meetings, I can attest to the fact that sharing your product plan as the lead topic is a terrible practice. Leading with a peek into what's bubbling under the hood will limit discussion. That's not good when your first order of business is to understand the customer's plans. Yes, sharing your road map is important, and it has its place—in the second half of the meeting. Never lead with your own agenda.

No, the first order of business and the true goal of an alignment meeting is reflected in a less well-known quotation from Jobs. He said, "You've got to start with the customer experience and work back toward the technology—not the other way around."

Exactly. The key to aligning with customers is first and foremost learning what they are trying to do. That's how you create an atmosphere of collaborative exploration. You and your team start by uncovering the customer's objectives. Only after understanding what the customer is trying to achieve and discovering what challenges they see before them does it make sense to discuss possible solutions you might offer at some time in the future. If anyone on your team fails to understand this, you risk talking about your company's plans before the customer is ready to hear what you have to say. If this happens, you may not hear the full story from the customer. To understand why, let's discuss the primary purposes of these meetings.

The four main objectives of a customer alignment meeting are ...

1. Uncover crucial customer information, specifically their goals and challenges.

2. Build customer relationships.

3. Remain open to client perspectives and stand ready to incorporate them into forward-looking plans.

4. Document and disseminate information to stakeholders.

We'll get into more detail on each of these later. Once you and your teammates are adept at all four, you will find yourselves making more informed decisions and planning better products, because you'll understand what your customers are trying to do.

Even if we think we know what direction we want to go, it's best to talk to customers. They're the experts when it comes to describing their goals and obstacles. And that's precisely the information you want to uncover. As longtime Microsoft CEO Steve Ballmer said, "We can believe that we know where the world should go. But unless we're in touch with our customers, our model of the world can diverge from reality. There's no substitute for innovation, of course, but innovation is no substitute for being in touch either."

ORDER MATTERS

A customer alignment meeting is a face-to-face conversation among your company's brain trust, the ones who create products and implement new strategies, and a client or customer who is a big source of revenue. The group discusses their plans and then assesses where there is alignment and where there are differences.

Broadly speaking, there are four major steps. The first is the uncovering session. This is when the team uncovers the customer's goals and challenges. Once the whole story has been understood, then, and only then, does the team move on to the second session, the road map. This is when the team of subject matter experts shares and discusses their plans. Having just heard the customer's story, they now have the knowledge necessary to focus on topics relevant to the customer. After discussing existing plans, the team can carve out smaller deep-dive discussions on any number of topics. Last is the wrap-up.

The order is intentional, and you are advised to adhere to it. Your meeting agenda will look like this:

1. Uncovering customer goals and challenges

2. Road map presentations

3. Deep dives

4. Wrap-up

Start with uncovering, and you'll quickly assess what the customer cares about. You'll also note what they don't care about. You can use that information later, during your road map presentations and deep-dive discussions. At those stages, you'll focus on their "care-abouts" and spend less time on what they don't care about. You'll maintain their interest and seem professional, all because you uncovered their story first. It's a simple trick but extremely powerful.

If instead, you start with your interests, you risk discussing facets of your plans that don't apply to this particular client. Besides wasting precious time, you're effectively telling the customer that you care more about getting feedback on your plans than you do about understanding their story. If you talk too much about your plans first, you risk alienating them. *Telling* before *listening* deteriorates their interest and confidence in you. That's precisely what you don't want.

Practically speaking, for an all-day customer alignment meeting, this means you might spend the first two hours uncovering the customer's ambitions and intentions, ninety minutes on your road map, two hours in deep-dive sessions, and thirty minutes to an hour on the wrap-up.

Now that we're clear on the ordering of the agenda, let's dive into the *why*, *where*, *who*, and *what* of customer alignment meetings—what they are and how they're put together.

WHY

Imagine that your company, "Q Corp," develops widgets. Your product planning department wants to assess whether plans for next-generation widgets will win the future business of target customers. Or your product planning team has no clue what direction to go for the next-generation products. Either way, the team needs to get in touch with target customers. This is where customer alignment meetings come in.

The purpose is simple: to learn the customer's goals and challenges and to discuss your company's road map. This informs the customer of what's bubbling under the hood and provides an opportunity to receive much-needed customer insights.

WHERE

Ideally, customer alignment meetings take place at your own company's headquarters. Video conference calls can work, but they're less desirable. It's difficult to establish a personal human connection over a call. Face-to-face meetings allow genuine connections to develop.

On occasion, a meeting might take place at the customer's office. However, it's preferable to conduct them at the host company's site because that allows your team to manage the event. As topics come up, you can call in the resident experts—especially when they work in the same building. Even on a video call, hosted at company headquarters, local subject matter experts can be called into the video conference as needed.

If yours is a multinational corporation that has offices spanning the globe, hosting a customer alignment meeting may present a logistical challenge. In this case, you may need to break the meeting into many separate discussions over video conference call. Try your best to arrange them around one topic at a time and focus on accommodating the key attendees. This is a case where meticulous note-taking is critical because many people will want to understand the outcome of meetings they could not attend.

Having the meeting at your own headquarters is optimal. It breaks customers away from their day-to-day environments and may shake them into a less guarded disposition. Being away from their desks, they may think about their goals and challenges from a new and unfettered perspective. They're free to think at a higher level or take a wider view. They may gain new insights into what they're trying to achieve.

WHO (FROM THE CUSTOMER COMPANY)

Let's imagine that fifty client companies regularly purchase your widgets. Executive staff has decided that in the future, your company will serve environmental and clean energy markets. They've identified five of these fifty clients as being representative of this market. These five companies account for a large percentage of revenue. Some develop disruptive technologies, and a few develop niche products that your team believes will become mainstream in a few years. You therefore schedule five separate customer alignment meetings, one with each company. This will give you five pulse readings of the overall market.

But who to specifically invite? This is when you remember Gilligan and the Professor. Invite the Professors, not the Gilligans.

Ideal customer attendees are people who know their business and markets. They command influence within their companies and sometimes across their industries. They understand why they need your expertise, whether for widgets in this case, legal advice in another, or advertising strategy in another. They also have a clear idea of what they're trying to do.

But how do you find that person? It takes work. Good old networking comes in handy. Sometimes you simply need to get out among your colleagues and talk to people until you find the right ones. A good place to start is with your direct sales force, if you have one. Ask them to help you find the Professor. If they're worth their salaries, they've constructed an organizational chart that tracks influence and knowledge. Give them guidance. Tell them what you're trying to achieve in the customer alignment meeting. Ask them to recommend people who have knowledge, influence, and vision. Or perhaps you don't have a sales department, but one of the partners in your law firm works with a client at issue and has a deep knowledge about the personalities on the other side. If your company builds components, ask for system architects. If you launch digital ad campaigns, seek out the best-connected marketing managers. Be willing to have a few business lunches to get the skinny on who to target. Whatever it takes, find the key personnel who influence the target customer company's road map. And then have that Professor bring along his or her right-hand trusted advisers, regardless of title, to the alignment meeting.

WHO (FROM YOUR OWN COMPANY)

Attendees from the host company should be well-regarded subject matter experts who have read this book or undergone training developed from it.

Do not invite anyone who does not understand the aligning skills and methods. I'm not saying this to sell more books. Honest. I'm saying this because it's critical that everyone on the team work from the same playbook. Otherwise, things can go downhill fast.

The roles of those on the aligning team include demonstrating credibility, asking skillful questions, listening attentively, taking verbatim notes, and genuinely striving to understand the customer's story.

Product planners, engineers, strategic business account managers, and executives all have roles in a customer alignment meeting for a technology firm. In an ad agency, the roster might include creative directors and project managers, while a pharmaceutical company would want to include their research scientists alongside the most respected regional manager of drug reps. The key is to invite a mix of expert product people and knowledgeable business folks who are adept in understanding the markets and the profit-and-loss statement. This is tricky, as often their interests are disparate or even conflicting. But never fear! If they all understand the goal of a customer alignment meeting and are well versed in skills of aligning, they'll work together like a well-oiled machine.

HOW MANY ATTENDEES?

When planning a customer alignment meeting, make sure you don't invite too many people from either side. If the ratio of people from your company is too high for every customer attendee, customers can feel overwhelmed or intimidated. When the room is too full, the dynamics turn into more of a one-way presentation than a forthright discussion. You want the forthright discussion. So make sure to manage the head count.

The rules of thumb for the right head count are 1:5, 2:7, 3:8.

1:5. If a single customer is visiting for the day, each session of the meeting should include no more than five internal employees for a total head count of six.

2:7. If a marketing manager brought along his trusted digital app designer, the customer head count is two. With two customers in attendance, it may be okay to invite a couple more internal attendees. Indeed, you may feel pressure to invite more as the second customer may want to discuss additional topics beyond what the first customer would.

3:8. As the number of customer attendees grows to three, the set of topics to be discussed may balloon. In that case, you may be tempted to invite a wide number of internal attendees. Again, be careful. Once the head count grows beyond ten, it's no longer a collaborative environment. People become more self-conscious and less forthright. The tendency is for one or two people to dominate the conversation as everyone else shrinks back.

Take care here. Only invite people if they'll add value to the meeting. In other words, each and every attendee must be filling a role. If they aren't, do not invite them. Notes will be taken. These other people can read the notes when they're distributed internally within a day or two after the meeting.

That said, be adaptable. Not every meeting is alike. If a bombastic CEO is attending, book a big room and let them have the floor in front of a wider audience for an hour before moving to another room with a smaller crew. Conversely, you may have invited a shy subject matter expert. In this case, reduce the head count further so that the customer doesn't feel put on the spot.

Keeping a lid on the head count can be difficult, but it's worth doing. Sometimes there is a lot of internal interest in attending. If head count is too high, you must turn down people. To assuage those who feel they need to take part, you can invite them to attend the premeeting, so they can nominate specific questions to be asked. Ask them to attend the follow-up meeting to hear directly from the team what was discussed. And make sure they receive the meeting notes.

For all-day meetings, which was our standard format, you can consider managing headcount by inviting different people into different sessions. But be careful not to turn it into a parade of different people coming and going. Balance consistency of attendees and manageable head count. Make sure every attendee shows up at the beginning for introductions and to hear the customer's presentation. Then they can leave, to return at a later time for their topic of interest. It takes a bit of juggling. But that is preferable to having too many people in the room during the sessions, where you want to roll up your sleeves and get into productive discussions.

The time you put into determining the right attendees and managing the head count will pay off many times over when you hold a customer alignment meeting with just the right people and just the right amount. Skimp on managing head count at your peril.

WHAT

The purpose of a customer alignment meeting is simple: to learn the customer's goals and challenges within their market and for their next-generation products or services. In order to discover these, the team simply learns techniques rooted in the concepts of active listening (described in depth in subsequent chapters).

With this format, it doesn't take much time for a customer alignment meeting to turn into a nitty-gritty discussion, an airing of conflicting opinions, or a brainstorming session of wide-ranging ideas. This is what we want—but this kind of forum can be fraught with hazards. So much so that I've known people who would prefer to avoid these meetings altogether. However, through the method of active listening, the road can be navigated and catastrophe avoided. By the end of the meeting, relationships may be stronger and the aligning team may have a better understanding of what the customers are trying to do. It's entirely worth doing, if done right.

To avoid danger, it can help to understand what customer alignment meetings are not.

First of all, let's be clear: a CA meeting is not a focus group. Focus groups tend to include many customers in one room led by a single host. The purpose of the discussion is to tease out people's subjective beliefs and reactions toward brands, products, or political messaging. Focus groups are formed in order to identify deep-seated feelings and associations. While it might make for enjoyable conversation, this kind of approach would be odd in a CA meeting.

CA meetings are not the place for sales pitches, nor are they a place to resolve current issues. If either of those things needs to happen, handle it well beforehand. Outstanding issues and education about new offerings should be dealt with prior to discussing futures.

Nor are CA meetings the place to showcase one's vast knowledge and awesomeness (aka indulge in chest-thumping). It's not a forum for describing internecine challenges, nor for airing dirty laundry, nor for bad-mouthing one's competition. It's never appropriate to tell customers information about their competitors, whether their competitors are your clients or not. (In fact, depending on your industry, you may not even take on competitors as clients.)

CA meetings are a place for learning customer goals and challenges and then for assessing how those goals and challenges line up with your team's road maps.

WHEN

Ideally, these meetings should be annual or semiannual affairs. One-off customer alignment meetings are marginally useful. At worst, they damage relationships. At best, they result in a few useful data points. For one thing, a single meeting might not provide enough time to hear the whole customer story. For another, customers could walk away expecting an ongoing relationship. This sets them up to feel jilted when they find that years later your company has failed to reconnect.

With respect to a single customer attendee, I found a good frequency for CA meetings to be every nine to eighteen months. This periodicity will heavily depend on the nature of your business and your own product cycles, so adjust as needed. At Altera, a semiconductor developer, our product cycle was about every two years. So meeting customers at least twice during the cycle worked well. By meeting frequently, we struck collegial connections with our customers. Conversations went deeper, and everyone involved developed broad and meaningful understandings of our customers' stories. Meeting more often than twice per cycle would have been odd, however, as development plans didn't change that quickly. Of course, your industry will have its own rhythms to take into account.

By meeting regularly, participants maintain a continuity of communication that makes subsequent meetings easy. The group simply continues the conversation from last time, updates each other with new information, and dives into details quickly.

Last, by meeting regularly, customers feel they aren't talking into a black hole. They are put at ease because they know they'll hear updates in future meetings and learn how their inputs were digested in the interim.

DURATION

Our typical customer alignment meetings lasted a full day. Starting over breakfast around 9:00 a.m., we'd either work through lunch or break for lunch and then finish up in the afternoon, sometime between 3:00 p.m. and 6:00 p.m.

That said, the duration is flexible. I've held meetings that were as short as three hours and others that lasted three days. It all depends on the number of attendees, number of topics, complexity of products, distance traveled, frequency of the meetings, and customer availability.

Our company was based in San Jose, California. For customers who were based nearby, we might meet with two engineers from a customer division once every nine months for three hours at a time. Other customers flew in from Europe or Asia. Depending on the number of attendees and topics, these CA meetings could involve breakout sessions over the span of multiple days. In the evenings, we'd take customers to dinner. Sometimes, when their stays spanned a weekend, the sales teams would take them hiking, wine tasting, golfing, fishing, or skiing. I've not got a strong opinion here on extracurricular activities. You do you.

THE WHO–WHAT–WHERE SUMMED UP

Every minute of preparation pays dividends in the quality and outcome of a customer meeting. If the right people are invited, all attendees understand what's expected of them, and your team starts the meeting earnestly striving to understand the customer's path forward, you'll have a successful meeting. Start with uncovering the customer's story and then dive into the details of other topics. Follow this order, and people will leave your meetings feeling their time was well spent. Most important, your team will have uncovered critical customer information that matters.

CHAPTER FOUR

Goals

"I hope I didn't bore you too much with my life story."
—Elvis Presley

THE ALIGNING TEAM'S GOAL

IN EVERY CUSTOMER ALIGNMENT MEETING, the single most important goal is to see the world from the customer's perspective.

Your goal when attending is to uncover the customer's goals and challenges. If your team understands this one concept and approaches it with curiosity, even if they forget everything else, you'll still be at an advantage over others who have never read this book. You'll be in alignment with the rest of your team, since you'll all be pursuing the same objective.

Understanding customers' objectives is critical to future planning. You can't do much with a singular request for a new product feature. You can't do much with an out-of-context improvement request, with no understanding of why the customer is requesting such a thing. If all you have are one-off requests, you will have no clue what customers will want from you in the future. When you take the time to understand the customer's view of the world as if you were in their shoes, you gain critical insights that can inform your activities: from small implementation-level decisions to big-picture strategies. Taken together, full stories from multiple customer perspectives form a tapestry of inputs critical to planning future products.

I'm reminded of many internal development planning meetings between us in the planning department and our colleagues in the engineering department. Their job was to design, develop, manufacture, test, and produce the products we were proposing to build. Engineers who accepted every line item without pushing back were rarer than profligate CEOs; they didn't exist. No, the modus operandi was to challenge each and every line item in our planning documents.

It was in these meetings where I was most thankful I understood the full context of customers' objectives as well as I did. Sometimes, I'd invited these very same engineers to CA meetings, where they'd heard firsthand what customers were trying to do. By being clear on what customers were trying to achieve, we put ourselves in a position to sensibly trade off implementation options as a team.

If, on the other hand, my knowledge had been limited to a simple laundry list of customer requests and I'd never invited any product developers to meet with customers directly, we'd have been lost. I wouldn't have been able to justify any of the requests, and the product definition would have gotten watered down to a point where it might not have addressed any markets.

Uncovering customer goals gives you the story, not just data points.

Customer demands can come in fast. On one hand, these discrete requests are simple to comprehend. However, when they come without context, they quickly become meaningless or, worse, fodder for bad decision-making.

When you ask customers to share their experiences and objectives, you learn their stories, and their requests suddenly have a context. If you collect enough of these stories, you start to get an idea of what directions they are going in. You begin to put together schemas or generalized frameworks of what your best and most insightful customers are trying to do. Suddenly, specific requests can be understood in the context of customer or client objectives. The reasons for pursuing new directions become easier to explain to your colleagues because you can tell the whole story to decision makers within the company.

Misguided Agendas

In the absence of this clearly defined goal for the uncovering team, individuals tend to pursue their own ad hoc, even if well-intentioned, agendas. They flit from topic to topic with no real strategy. Here are examples of some misguided agendas I've witnessed. They have no place in customer alignment meetings:

- collecting answers to specific questions when they don't apply to the customer;
- fishing for specific data to justify some project;
- solving current technical problems;
- pitching current products or road maps;
- spreading fear, uncertainty, and doubt about competitors;
- taking on unnecessary action items; and
- educating customers.

Problems may arise that need solving. Or you may realize the customer is unaware of currently available technology that may help them with a technical challenge. A CA meeting, *especially the first half*, is not the correct time to address such things. The right time is in another meeting, or at some point after the initial uncovering session.

There are a couple of reasons why CA meetings shouldn't focus on resolving specific issues. For one, if you jump on these topics too early, the customer may believe you've solved all their problems. In this case, you've robbed them of the incentive to tell you their goals and challenges. They may get the impression that you've already made all their dreams come true. If that's the case, why should they tell you anything more? This is the last thing you want! Don't derail the conversation by solving current problems.

By solving tactical problems in the same CA meeting, you are setting misguided expectations for customers. You're effectively telling them that when they attend CA meetings, they are getting a team of top experts and executives to accelerate and prioritize their problems then and there. Not only will you subvert normal processes for issue resolution, but your subsequent CA meetings may have the customer going through the motions of appearing to fill your goals merely as the price to be paid for problem prioritization. This might become their only reason for attending onsite. The customer might leave happy, but you'll likely walk away with low-quality information.

Take care to stick to the objectives of the CA meeting. Don't mix in other objectives, or you risk diluting your results.

Start with uncovering customer goals and challenges.

After introductions, the first order of business is to uncover customer goals and challenges. This may seem awkward or rude. You may think you need to present your road map first, simply out of courtesy, or to not put the customer on the spot. But here's the thing: if you fail to first diagnose what the customer is trying to do, you may waste everyone's time talking about plans in the works that are irrelevant in the customer's world.

If you spend too much time talking about subject matters that customers don't care about, they'll lose interest. Once you've lost connection with the customer, the meeting is wasted. So, for now, put aside strategy, products, or services you want to discuss. Start by learning what the customer is trying to do as well as what obstacles the customer is trying to overcome. Only after this full story has been heard, restated, confirmed, and understood is it appropriate for you to discuss anything else. Only after you know what the customer cares about is it time for you to share *your* game plans, technology under development, or solutions.

This can feel awkward. Maybe a customer starts describing a solution they need, a solution that your team has already developed and delivered to the market. The obvious reaction is to share the information.

Bad move. What happens next? The attendee stops talking and sharing, since this has been deemed resolved. That's unfortunate, because the entire point of the meeting is to listen to her.

Instead, ask questions to understand why the customer wants the functionality she is requesting. Your team should seek to uncover the nature of the product the customer is building, if you're in the tech industry, or what the new product being launched is, if you're an ad agency meeting with a key brand. By providing a ready-wrapped solution, the team forfeits any chance of understanding what the customer is trying to accomplish. What's the point of a CA meeting if the team discourages the customer from talking? But that's precisely what happens when the team presents solutions prior to diagnosing the customer's full story.

Start by looking into the crystal ball.

Notice again what we're after: the customer's goals and challenges. These are future-looking and aspirational. You want to know the customer's road map—where they're headed and why. It may feel awkward to start asking about the future when you haven't discussed the current situation. Even so, start in the future. Don't worry. As you ask future-looking questions, the customer won't be able to stop himself from filling in details about his current circumstances. However, if you start with questions about the current situation, you'll find yourself mired in the here and now. You can't change the here and now. You want to learn what the customer is trying to achieve, so you can develop the tools that she will want to use in the future. So start in the future.

As Wayne Gretzky famously said, you want to skate to where the puck is heading, not to where it has been. So ask where they're aiming their pucks. This meeting is called a "customer alignment meeting" for a reason: you want to align road maps. That's impossible unless you know where the customer's strategy is aimed.

Uncover goals and challenges in the realm of the *customer's* expertise.

Keep the conversation in the realm of the *customer's* expertise. You want to talk about what they're trying to achieve, not to learn their opinions of how you should design your product. They're not experts in your company's technological trade-offs or in details of your operational or budgetary constraints. Those are your concerns. So don't ask them for their opinions on such matters.

This can be tricky to navigate. Once they get going, customers can sometimes barrage you with an unending list of unrealistic demands. A common reaction is to play defense and reply with your own list of tremendous challenges that prevent you from implementing what they ask for. The thing is, your technology is typically not within the realm of the customer's expertise. Rather than focusing on the nitty-gritty details of implementing a particular solution, instead get the customer talking about why they require such features. Ask them what they are trying to accomplish. That's their area of expertise. Stay on their side of the road. A line of questioning that keeps them talking about their own motivations will get you valuable information that can guide your planning efforts.

To say it another way, when you feel backed into a corner, defending your design trade-offs, it's time to turn it around and ask questions to uncover what the customer is trying to do. Use the feeling of defensiveness as a trigger. Remember to put the questions back on the customer, to ask what they're trying to accomplish or what's motivating their concerns about your implementation details. It may feel like descending deeper into the abyss, but I assure you, climbing down is often the way out. (Thanks to *30 Rock*'s Jack Donaghy for this bit of wisdom.)

Uncover *all* the customer's goals and challenges, not just one.

Note that the alignment team's goals are plural. They are to uncover all customer goals and customer obstacles, not just one. The customer may have three lofty goals and five looming, pernicious, and terrifying obstacles in their way. Uncover them all. Don't worry. I'll explain precisely how to do this in the aligning skills chapters.

Gauge the importance of each goal.

When customers have multiple goals, it can be overwhelming to understand which ones matter the most. Which do you focus on?

There's a neat, simple trick to assess this: ask them their cost of inaction. Ask what would happen if they did nothing or if you did nothing. Ask what would happen if they tried but failed to achieve a goal. The answer will tell you how important the goal or challenge is.

For example, the customer might answer, "If we do nothing, we'll lose market share to our competitor." In this case, you know it's somewhat important but may not be dire. However, if the customer says, "We'll be out of our jobs," then you know this goal is of supreme importance. But don't stop there. Strive to quantify the cost. Who will they be losing their market share to? How big is that market with respect to their overall revenue? If you think these questions are too personal or will move the conversation in the wrong direction, then save them for later. But do ask.

To be fair, everything your customer tells you is important. However, that can result in a large data set. Teasing out the most substantial pieces gives you insight into context and priority. Knowing the cost of inaction is a good shortcut to getting an idea of the relative significance of each goal and challenge. Assessing the relative importance of each goal and each challenge is so valuable that you'll carve out time to make sure your understanding is correct at the end of the day.

Patience is an asset.

Often we walk into meetings with our heads full of questions and we want to ask them straightaway. Be patient! Your first order of business is to uncover the customer story. Later in the day, perhaps after lunch, you'll have your chance to pose your burning questions. After all, only after you've fully uncovered the customer's story is it appropriate to ask any questions that do not directly elicit the customer's goals and challenges.

In the course of uncovering, you may find that after the customer has shared the full story, only a few questions haven't been answered. Wait for the appropriate time to ask them. Work with the team lead to identify when this is. At the very least, wait until the team has learned all the customer goals and challenges before even thinking about asking detailed and self-centered questions. If you ask these too soon, the customer might stop being so forthright. Why? Because the message you're sending is that all you care about is your narrow set of questions or selling your narrow set of products. It's selfish. The customer needs to be heard before they'll listen.

What success looks like.

A customer alignment meeting is successful if, at the end, you can answer these kinds of questions from the customer's viewpoint:

1. What is the customer trying to achieve? What are their goals? For example: What market are they going after? What product are they attempting to develop? For what market need? What criteria do their customers care about and why? Where do their customers see value, and which "table stake" features are required without question (in other words, which features are 100 percent required and so obvious the customer might not even mention them)? If you are at all unsure whether the visiting company cares about these "table stakes," wait until the second part of the meeting and confirm these requirements then.

2. What are the challenges the customer sees in their way? What obstacles will they need to overcome to deliver a winning result in their marketplace? How are their competitors positioning themselves? What governmental factors must they work with?

This sounds easy enough, but beware. We all come to meetings with our own agendas and interests. Your colleague might be working on a project where an implementation decision needs to be made by the end of the day. The sheer urgency of their responsibilities might prompt them to rapid-fire questions about that specific issue at the earliest perceived opportunity in the meeting. If they don't know that uncovering the customer's story must happen first or if they don't know what the uncovering team's goals are, they might take over the conversation at the wrong time and deny the customer the chance of being heard. Your team will thus fail to uncover the information that matters. This is why it's critical that everyone on the team work from the same playbook, agree on common goals, and follow the proper order of the meeting.

CHAPTER FIVE

Mind-Set

"The first and simplest emotion which we discover in the human mind, is curiosity." —Edmund Burke

UNLEASH THE TODDLERS

Arranging the logistics of a customer alignment meeting is one thing. Creating the proper mind-set is another.

Let's start by considering a toddler. Yes, maybe some of your colleagues act like toddlers. But I'm not talking about them. No. Think of an actual two- to three-year-old toddler. A consistent attitude is that of curiosity. Toddlers can't help themselves—dropping objects to see how they land or pulling open drawers to see what's inside. Toddlers are forever experimenting and exploring in an effort to understand the world around them. In this quest, they're fearless and unrelenting.

As we age, the fortunate among us retain our sense of curiosity, even if moving our attention to more cerebral topics such as the flow of electrons in semiconductor materials or the flow of money in an economy.

For others, curiosity dulls with age. With exploration can come failure, and with failure can come pain. And so we stop trying, merely to avoid hurting ourselves. Or perhaps novelty becomes elusive and boredom supplants curiosity. Whatever the reason for its absence, a lack of curiosity among attendees almost always leads to disappointing results.

Besides being tedious, discussions in such meetings amount to people practically talking to themselves. They ask questions they already know answers to or drone on about things they already know.

Genuine curiosity is required fuel for the concepts contained in this book. The tactics of aligning don't go far if implemented half-heartedly. They're much more effective when practiced by people who are genuinely curious to learn the customer's perspective.

If curiosity doesn't come naturally, try to kindle it. You can try seeking out novelty. Here are some ways to cultivate curiosity:

- Don't focus on what you want to learn. Instead, ask yourself how the customer sees the world.

- Try to identify specific ways that the customer's view of the world differs from yours.

- Rather than focusing on what you're trying to achieve with your current projects, strive to understand what the customer is trying to achieve.

- Rather than focusing on what issues you face in your job, strive to understand what obstacles your customer is trying to navigate.

Later, in the skills chapters, we'll review more ways to cultivate curiosity in a CA meeting. Of utmost importance is to clear your mind of your own concerns before opening the door to the meeting and then walk into the room with an attitude of curiosity and openness. Get out of your own head and shift your perspective to that of the customer. You'll find novelty here. Your innate curiosity may pop back to life. Once it appears, let it drive you.

THE ALIGNING TEAM'S MIND-SET

The proper mind-set of the alignment team, first and foremost, is of genuine curiosity. This means starting with the customer's story and understanding it as well as possible by crafting questions that elicit thoughtful and honest responses. The team must strive to be fully present with its attention. Thoughts and perceptions should be unhindered by bias, corporate constraints, or misguided agendas. But how to reach this mythical state?

Clear your mind.

We play a central role in our own storylines. We've lived them for so long, it can be difficult to assume another's perspective. But that's precisely what your job is in a customer alignment meeting. Put aside your own mental clutter. Then simply strive to understand the customer's storyline from his or her perspective. Don't worry. After the meeting has ended, you're welcome to pop back to your own perspective.

This sounds easy, but it can be difficult and even scary. Our discursive minds generate thoughts. We like to latch on to these thoughts, sometimes as if they are a part of us, as if they define us. Letting such thoughts go can feel like a loss of control or a loss of self. For many, this is not a pleasant feeling. I assure you, however, that if you develop the ability to let go your own thoughts, the perspectives of others will become much clearer to you.

I can advise "put your thoughts aside before entering the meeting," and intellectually you might agree to do so, but carrying this out can be a monumental task. It takes mindfulness, training, and an ability to step away from being the center of your universe. This chapter provides some tricks for adopting this clear-eyed mind-set.

Write down your agenda and then physically put it aside.

Writing down your agenda, as well as top-of-mind questions, frees you from remembering all these loose ends so that you can fully focus on the customer's story.

At one point in my career, I was planning products where I needed to understand embedded memory requirements in detail. I had decisions to make, based on what customers wanted in terms of access speeds, bandwidth rates, memory sizes, word sizes, power, etc. Before meetings, I would write down these questions and then set them aside. This simple act removed any need to keep them at the top of my mind. After all, they were right there for me to refer to at any time. It freed me to fully focus on what the customer was saying.

After the customer had fully shared his story and during the appropriate session, I would review my questions. The upshot, of course, was that by that point, having heard the customer's story, I was in a position to know which questions were relevant. Then I'd ask them.

Check your ego.

When you're in a customer alignment meeting, establishing credibility for your team before the client is important, especially if you're an appointed expert. But the way to do so isn't by peacocking and strutting about with your résumé of accomplishments. When it's your turn to introduce yourself, briefly . . .

- explain what you are responsible for within the company;

- bullet point a couple of relevant credentials;

- identify a project you're working on; and

- state what you hope to get out of the meeting.

Use as few words as possible. Try to drop just a few industry-specific words or comments that let the customer know you're familiar with their technology, business, or market. This may sound like a lot of information to convey, but when done right, it should take no more than a minute or two. After you've accomplished this, relinquish the spotlight and don't try to prove anything or flaunt your bona fides.

Let go of fear, corporate edicts, and technical constraints.

As an expert, you may bristle at hearing what seem to be unrealistic desires or expectations from clients and customers. You may want to bring these dreams closer to earth. By hearing these requests without objecting, you may feel you are communicating a tacit commitment to deliver whatever the customer describes. Staying silent may feel impossible. Correcting the customer might feel necessary. But hold on! There's a way through this, I assure you.

Imagine that your company has been clamping down on costs. Executives have decided to halt all developments in the area the customer cares about. How could you possibly sit there and listen to the customer talk about what's wanted, when you know that your company will not deliver what's being asked for?

The answer is to move the conversation back to what the customer is trying to do and the customer's area of expertise: their goals and challenges. Your area of expertise certainly will have all kinds of constraints. You're steeped in these realities day in and day out. It's almost impossible to put them aside when you're talking to a customer. But put them aside you must. Otherwise you'll only see the customer's perspective through your own filter of constraints, fear, and preconceived notions. To come up with the right plans, you need to experience the world from the customer's perspective, not yours. I know it's difficult, even frustrating. The first step is acknowledging you have your own perspective. Then, do everything you can to shed it, for a few hours at least, using these tips. Gently nudge the customer back to their side of the street. You can start by striving to learn exactly what's motivating their request.

Cultivate a compassionate nature.

Cultivating compassion is the first step in seeing the world from another's perspective. Straightaway, as the meeting begins, it can be helpful to set a deliberate intention to learn what the world looks like from the customer's vantage point.

As shifting your perspective is not a straightforward exercise, consider reading the book *Nonviolent Communication: A Language of Life* by Marshall B. Rosenberg. (You'll find this and other recommended reading in the appendix.) In his introduction, Rosenberg describes the first time he was bullied by a classmate. Despite the hurt he felt, his primary reaction was curiosity. He wondered why the bully was behaving that way and how he could maintain a compassionate nature, even while feeling attacked so that he could still regard his attacker as human.

He cites a more extreme case, that of Etty Hillesum, a Jewish woman who kept a journal while supporting fellow Jews passing through a Nazi transit camp during World War II. In that journal, she described how she maintained compassion for the German guards, even as they yelled at her. Instead of focusing on their words or how their tone hurt her, she looked into them, deeper. With compassion, she saw human beings struggling with frustration and anger.

She wondered about their childhoods or their struggles with relationships. She saw them as suffering humans rather than cruel monsters. She longed to help them work through their issues.

The lesson here is that despite having her own problems, not the least of which was being confined and starved in a concentration camp, Hillesum was still able to move her point of perspective to that of a compassionate observer. Despite being directly affected by the behavior of the young man in front of her, she retained composure, curiosity, and compassion. Obviously, you're not in nearly as dire a situation, but her example is instructive. If Hillesum could empathize with her jailers, surely we can empathize with our customers.

Imagine a scenario where you feel attacked by a customer. In response, your instinct might be to focus on your own story and grow defensive. If instead you turn your attention to the customer's story with a genuine attitude of curiosity, you might turn the conversation around. You would be able to discover the reasons behind the customer's requests, rather than being annoyed that the requests were being made. This is how you "get back to the customer's side of the street."

It's all fine and good to understand that your job is to uncover customer goals and challenges. Until you cultivate a compassionate nature, however, you may find your own thought processes getting in the way. Unless you are able to put aside your agenda and constraints and focus on those of the customer, you may find yourself in defensive positions. Once there, you risk being deaf to what's really being said.

So when you feel you're being attacked by a customer making unrealistic demands, remember Etty Hillesum or little Marshall Rosenberg. If they could cultivate compassion for their abusers, so can you for a customer who cares enough about your product to travel to you and dedicate an entire day to discussing your road maps together. Focus on customers, and let curiosity guide you in learning about their situation.

Put on your detective's hat.

This may sound corny, but in my experience, by the simple act of imagining you're a detective, you'll find it easier to shed your own agendas. If it helps you to get in the right mind-set, imagine you're none other than the masterful Sherlock Holmes, hot on a case to solve the greatest mystery of all: the customer's unique situation. Dispassionately collect clues, ask probing questions, and assemble a picture of truth.

Sure, this imagery may feel silly. But if it works, who cares?

Your job is simple. It's no longer to plan products, create ads, or do whatever else your day job requires, but rather to unearth clues. Once your detective hat is on, it's easier to step into the world from the customer's perspective.

For practice or if you're skeptical, try it out on family and friends. Or put on your imaginary detective's hat with colleagues. Do remember: smoking a pipe is not legal in most workplaces.

Cultivate a growth mind-set.

An open-minded attitude where you continuously seek to learn is the best type of mind-set to bring to a meeting. People with growth mind-sets believe that anything can be learned. They regard failures as learning opportunities. They let curiosity lead them, whether they look foolish or not. In fact, looking foolish scarcely matters to people with a growth mind-set. Their objective is to learn and be enlightened, not to protect their image of themselves or of their work.

The book *Mindset* by Carol Dweck compares two ways of thinking: fixed mind-sets versus growth mind-sets. In a fixed mind-set, a person believes that achievement comes from natural ability and that failure is an indication of ineptitude. In this mind-set, the entire world is a judge and eyes are constantly evaluating performance. People with fixed mind-sets strive to protect themselves from such judgment. As a result, they pursue experiences that bolster their self-esteem and avoid situations that may reveal incompetence. It keeps them stuck in their own perspectives and renders them unable to shift perspectives—for example, to the perspective of a customer.

Once you've adopted a growth mind-set, it's much easier to be compassionate, to put yourself in the customer's shoes. Besides, my dear Watson, detectives' hats fit only those heads that contain growth mind-sets and that's the hat you'll be wearing in all customer alignment meetings.

Reserve judgment.

You and your teammates are embarking on a delicate mission. Your goal is to learn what the customer is trying to achieve without leading them to the answer you want to hear or pushing them toward your own agendas. When you have a genuinely curious team, cultivating compassion and operating with growth mind-sets, and you have a team of people operating beyond their comfort zones, taking risks, and potentially asking questions that make them look stupid, that's okay.

Be gentle with one another. Rather than judge teammates to be idiots for asking questions that landed poorly, support them. After the customer alignment meeting, compliment them for taking a risk. Offer to review what happened and come up with strategies for improving together.

Later, you'll learn a questioning technique that makes someone on the team look deliberately foolish (on purpose). Realize that it takes real courage and a growth mind-set for a colleague to put herself or himself out to look like an idiot in front of coworkers. Make the team dynamic a safe one by reserving judgment. Use the postmeeting forum to review and improve. And move on when mistakes are made in the meeting itself.

Focus on the customer.

During the uncovering sessions, when you find yourself about to talk about *your* trade-offs or *your* product details, stop. A customer alignment meeting should be held in the customer's realm. Get back there as quickly as you can. Put on your detective's hat, think with a growth mind-set, tap into your compassion. Instead of explaining your constraints, ask your customer what exactly they think a specific feature request will do for them. What problem will it solve? What objective will it help them drive toward? Make it about the customer, not about you.

Focus on the future.

Start the customer alignment meeting by asking about future objectives. When you align two vectors, you need to know their direction. So ask about the customer's direction. Don't worry. They'll fill you in on relevant details about today's projects as they answer.

Keep those future-oriented questions flowing until you are absolutely sure you've uncovered the full story. You keep asking about your customer's future goals and challenges until they've shared everything. Only then is it okay to ask about today or, sparingly, about the past.

Customer aligning mind-set in a nutshell

Attendees should come to customer alignment meetings with open, growth-oriented, people-oriented, future-oriented, and customer-oriented mind-sets.

Yes, the team can bring presentations, questions they're dying to ask, and information to share. But it should all be put away until two key questions, *What are the customer's goals?* and *What are the customer's challenges?*, have been answered—in full. The first order of business is uncovering the customer's worldview. Until it is understood, all other business is to be put aside.

This includes preconceived opinions. For example, do you think cost is the main constraint customers care about? Are you looking to confirm that opinion? Don't. Put all thoughts of cost aside as you enter the meeting. Do you think all customers want higher performance, and even if they complain about high power, they'll find a way to work around it? Stop. Put that idea aside and pretend that you have no idea what customers want. With a tabula rasa mind-set, you will be more capable of uncovering the truth. Don't worry. You can bring your preconceived notions to the table in the latter part of the meeting.

CHAPTER SIX

How Not to Align

"Success depends upon previous preparation, and without such preparation there is sure to be failure." —Confucius

Imagine you've been invited to a customer alignment meeting, but you've skipped the training. You think, *No biggie. It's called a customer alignment meeting. What more information do I need? I'm no dumdum. I can wing this.*

In each scenario below, you are the lead character. You have a specific title and a certain perspective. Think through each example as if you are that person and ponder what's going on. Keep in mind the information from earlier about the purpose of aligning with customers. We will delve more into the desired aligning skills later. For now, let's see what it looks like when we all wing it.

SCENARIO 1: CUSTOMER ATTACKS!

You are the subject matter expert (SME) for a linchpin proprietary technology. It's at the core of your company's product portfolio. You find yourself in a customer alignment meeting, and the customer's chief engineer is talking. And, boy oh boy, is he talking. He rattles off one lofty pie-in-the-sky suggestion after another—all ideas for *you* to implement—as if it would be easy. He says he wants half the size, twice the performance, and half the price. Oh and, don't forget, the widget must implement the newfangled bizzy-whip protocol that everyone's jazzed about.

You try to maintain an expression of calm, but internally you're boiling with anger. This fool is untethered from reality. You're a talented engineer and, sure, you could deliver on one of these requests, maybe even two. But all of them? Impossible. It's not technically feasible. Simple as that. There are trade-offs to be made, not to mention the minor detail that you are bound by the laws of physics and a finite amount of financing!

Unbelievably, the meeting host encourages the customer to keep spewing unrealistic demands and the customer obliges. It's madness. You think of the to-do list sitting on your desk. It's already longer than you can comprehend, much less work your way through. Now you have to sit here as impossible demands are flung at you? The tenet "The customer is always right" crosses your mind, and you think, *No, in this case the customer's dead wrong.*

It seems that by indulging the customer like this, by allowing him to brainstorm unrestrained, the team is leading him on. It's as if the team is leading him to believe his wish is your command. Simply by listening to these unrealistic demands you're tacitly committing to delivering them, and you're not willing to sign up for any of it. It's an assault, and you cannot let it go on any longer.

What do you do?

You decide to set the customer straight. He needs to understand that his needs are about as realistic as building a machine to teleport people to Mars, even if, at this moment, you'd like very much to shove him into such a contraption.

During a brief pause, you interject. You explain, as gently as possible, how outrageous his requests are. You estimate the costs of each request and explain that he can either have one or another but not all. You go to the whiteboard and draw a diagram that shows how the architecture cannot possibly be made to bend to his requests. The product would have to be fully redesigned from the ground up, but then it'd cost many times more than he's currently paying.

He objects with some ideas for making it work. You anticipate and parry each idea. You explain that even if you designed it as he suggested, various other features that he's grown accustomed to would have to be cut or degraded in some unacceptable way. His proposals, if implemented, would burden other customers who did not want such features. You point out that none of his requests come for free. Even with half his requests, costs would skyrocket beyond price points he'd be willing to pay.

You're angry. You sound combative. But you're justified because his requests are outrageous. He demands the impossible and clearly does not appreciate the difficulty of your job or the complexity of your technology.

What happens next?

The customer apologizes and explains that he wasn't familiar with all your constraints. He sits back in his chair and turns his attention to the front of the room and waits for the host to continue the meeting. Within minutes, a colleague from the product planning department is reviewing slides that show details of the next-generation devices the company is planning to build—devices you've already agreed to design. Now the team is back on track, and you're getting feedback on real plans, not blue-sky pipe dreams. The customer answers the presenter's questions, even if with reduced enthusiasm.

You're satisfied, having gotten the meeting back on course.

But are you back on course? Nope. You're in deep trouble.

We'll refer to this scenario throughout the book, but briefly, here's the problem. When you argue with the customer, at every turn telling him why what he wants can't be done, you eventually kill his enthusiasm to share what he's trying to accomplish. He'll stop talking. The real problem here was the focus. By having the customer focus on what he wanted you to implement, you had him advising on a topic he was not an expert in.

It would be better to redirect the customer to discussing *his own* objectives. If the team had gotten him talking about his own project goals, rather than focusing on what he thought you needed to implement, you would have been gathering useful information that was within his area of expertise. You would have learned what was driving his need for a smaller device or for faster performance or whiz-bang whatnot features. Once you knew his underlying objectives, you could have had a productive conversation. Instead, you shut him down. You may feel you won. In reality, everyone lost.

SCENARIO 2: HORRIFIED LEGAL VICE PRESIDENT

You're the vice president of a legal firm that specializes in patent law and protection from lawsuits. You arrived early to a customer alignment meeting and struck up a conversation with the client. You discovered that you both attended the same university.

Remarkably, you're also both avid sailors. You swap tales of high seas adventures and reminisce about the elaborate pranks of alpha house. By the time the meeting begins, you've developed an amiable rapport.

The host, Bob, leads a round of introductions. He reviews the agenda, confirms that the agenda meets the customer's needs, and launches into a presentation titled "What We Heard Last Time." It's a bit cringe-worthy. It's a verbatim regurgitation, replete with quotes, of what this same customer said in a similar meeting a year before. *What a waste of time*, you think. *Obviously, the customer knows what he said last time he was here.* However, the customer looks comfortable, so you stay silent. The customer corrects Bob a few times. You suspect that Bob is out of his depth. You can't wait for the meeting to move on.

Soon, the customer is standing in front of a PowerPoint presentation. The order feels awkward to you; the team is putting the customer on the spot by making him present his plans first. It would be more polite to present your updates and then ask for the customer's feedback.

In any event, he has come prepared and his slides clearly convey what he's trying to achieve with his next-generation products. He reviews a diagram and explains what new features may be patentable as well as other features that may infringe on existing patents. A junior lawyer asks him what protocol he'll use between two devices in his diagram. You're horrified. Anyone who knows anything about this market would know the answer. It's a stupid question.

What do you do?

Embarrassed, you answer on the customer's behalf. "It's Interlaken," you say. And having followed the presentation so attentively, you volunteer, "With what, sixteen channels?" The customer nods in agreement. Satisfied, you glare at the junior partner and attempt to telepathically transmit *No more stupid questions.*

A few minutes later, a director from another department asks, "What do you see as the biggest challenges in your way?"

The customer nods slowly but remains silent. He pauses and looks up at the ceiling. *Oh boy*, you think, *we've put him on the spot now.* You can't stand it and so bail him out. You offer a suggestion. "You know, such things as uncertainty over which technology to embrace, shifting customer demand, an attack by patent trolls, those kinds of things."

The customer looks at you and considers for a moment. "Yeah, all of those I suppose." He returns his attention to his presentation.

Whew! Disaster averted. But not for long. The customer discusses three new inventions in depth. Another junior partner asks, "What are the 'new art' aspects of these new inventions?" You can't believe your ears! The customer just finished saying they already e-mailed the descriptions to the team. Anyone can read the invention disclosures and answer that question for themselves. You can't stand to let the customer answer such a stupid question, so you let the design engineer know what's what. Addressing the customer, you say, "I'm sorry, clearly not all of us have done our homework and read our briefs. I assure you we are up to snuff with what you've sent to us." The junior attorney looks down at his hands.

Incredibly, over the next half hour, every single question is embarrassingly stupid. Every time, you feel you must save the customer, so you answer on his behalf.

You think, *What a bunch of dopes this younger generation of patent lawyers are. Who hired these people?* You're embarrassed they're on your team, as they seem utterly immature, clueless, and unprofessional.

At the break, Bob, the host, approaches you in the hallway. You expect him to thank you for taking time out of your busy schedule to attend this client meeting. Instead, incredibly, he asks you to stop answering on behalf of the customer. It's outrageous. You say, "I'll tell you what, Bob. I'll stop answering as soon as people stop asking stupid questions."

Bob explains that there's no use in the customer being there if he's not allowed to answer for himself. Bob doesn't get it. You fire back, "I can tell by your questions that you don't know the first thing about this customer's product or technologies. Besides, who are *you* to tell me what to do?"

What went wrong?

Turns out, Bob was right. No matter how stupid a question seems, if it's directed at the customer, everyone on the team needs to let the customer answer. By bailing the customer out with a list of options or outright answering questions on the customer's behalf, you rob the team of an opportunity to learn the customer's story in his own words.

In these customer alignment meetings, everyone on the team must be comfortable with silence and willing to let the customer describe a full and useful answer, no matter how "stupid" the original questions may seem. More on this topic in the skills sections.

SCENARIO 3: TECHNICAL MARKETING ENGINEER SAVE

You're a technical marketing engineer responsible for the rollout and marketing of premium products. You craft marketing campaigns, develop supporting product collateral, and plan all accompanying software requirements.

The customer alignment meeting starts, and the meeting host asks the customer what her goals are for her next-generation product. Straightaway, she laments that the interfaces need to be nimbler. She explains that the software seemed to have been designed for high-bandwidth, large-burst data packets. But that's not what she wants. She's frustrated because they can't seem to design around it. They've tried various compiler settings and various gearbox modes. Having studied the circuit diagrams in the data book, she can see that what she wants to do is physically possible. However, the supporting software and out-of-the-box code don't give her the controls she needs to make use of the architecture.

You can't believe that your colleagues are remaining silent. You've got the answer to all her problems! Only a month ago, you put out a press release announcing a software download that provides precisely the tools she's describing. The patch includes a user mode that would allow her to do exactly what she wants.

What do you do?

You educate everyone, explaining what's included in the software patch, and point out that it's already available online. You pull out a business card. On the back, you write the full path to the directory and the file name, so she'll be sure to find it straightaway. As you hand her the card, you tell her to contact you if she runs into any problems. She thanks you. You look around the room to get congratulatory eye contact. You get mixed results. Never mind, you're a hero.

You note how passive everyone is being. No one's selling the customer on all the technology that's currently available. She could make use of it today, if she was only aware of it. You pull out a glossy product brochure and lay it on the middle of the table, facing her. You list each of the big sellers, explaining why they're popular with customers. She nods with appreciation.

Out of the blue, the host asks the customer to expand on her performance goals.

She explains that the device she's using is barely meeting timing and they have more functionality to add. She worries that they won't make their targets.

You ask what software build she's using, and she tells you.

"Oh," you say, "well, in the next software release you'll find a compile mode that optimizes the kinds of routes that are currently limiting you. We've found that the typical design sees performance gains of 20 percent. I imagine you should see some improvements there. You may want to upgrade to the latest build and check it out."

"Oh, okay," she says, scribbling in her notepad. You've saved the day. Problem solved.

She continues to the next item on the list of requests and complaints she's prepared for the meeting. "Well, then, I guess I'll move on to packaging. We're developing a handheld unit. A one millimeter ball pitch won't do. We need 0.8 millimeter."

Coincidentally, you're on the cross-functional packaging planning committee. Yet again you've got precisely the solution for her. "In three months we'll be introducing the part you're using, but in a package that is 60 percent smaller and with a ball pitch of 0.8 millimeter. It's ideal for handheld form factors."

"Oh, thanks. I'll let the team know," she says again, writing in her notepad. She thanks you and turns her attention back to the host. "I'm done."

You, too, look at the host, expecting a nod of appreciation. Instead, you receive an unfriendly glare. You're perplexed. Did he not just witness you coming to the rescue at every turn and solving all her problems? What on earth is going on?

What went wrong?

Much like the technical subject matter expert who parried every request and the vice president who answered on behalf of the customer, this is another example that shuts down the customer. By jumping so quickly and enthusiastically into problem-solving, you robbed the team of hearing the customer's story. Instead of giving the customer the space and time to give a full picture of what she was trying to do, you jumped to solve her problems. Once all the customer's problems were solved, what incentive did she then have to share her perspective?

Remember: learning customer goals and challenges is the main goal of customer alignment meetings, not solving current problems. Now imagine that soon after this meeting, an executive who didn't attend decides that this IP (intellectual property) patch, the one that solved the customer's problem, should be removed from the website. From the director's perspective, the patch has caused nothing but trouble because it's caused a spike in hotline calls. The director thinks the IP should be simplified or removed. That's the general sentiment within the company, and subordinates line up to support that view.

If all you knew was the customer had a problem that the patch solved, your case might be lost. On the other hand, if you understood the story behind her need for such functionality, you could create a substantiated rebuttal. The director could then make a strategic decision, instead of an ill-informed tactical mistake. You'd have a compelling story as to why this feature was important, not just a data point telling you that one customer needs it without any context at all. If you hadn't jumped in so quickly and, instead, had heard the customer's full story, your team might be able to come up with another workable solution. Knowing what the customer is trying to do is significantly more valuable than knowing that a customer wants a specific feature out of context.

SCENARIO 4: FINANCIAL PLANNER—THE HARD SELL

You've decided you need advice from a professional financial planner. You find yourself sitting at a small conference room with two planners. Tom assures you they'll have you on a solid financial path by the end of the day. Bob says he specializes in bespoke investments.

You explain that despite your best efforts to save, it seems you can't seem to pay off your credit cards.

Bob asks if you have any mutual funds. You say you do not.

Tom asks what assets you have. You mention your house and a small inheritance.

He then asks if you have a 401(k). You answer that you and your spouse have 401(k) retirement accounts but with small balances.

Bob asks whether you're familiar with the exciting new mutual fund family that his company has just introduced. You are not.

"Can I tell you a little more about my situation, before we get into those topics?" you ask. "We bring in $150k a year, but we have $30k in credit card debt, and the balance never seems to go down. We pay PMI on a mortgage, which, I don't know, maybe is a good thing, but it feels like a bad thing. I'm thirty-five, and at the end of each month I feel like more money goes out than comes in. It's stressful."

No one is taking notes.

Bob says, "When you first contacted us, you said something about an inheritance?"

"That's right. It's $60k and sitting in our savings account. I thought about paying off the credit cards but thought I should talk with you first."

"Paying off the cards is certainly one option," Bob says. "However, sometimes, having debt is good. You need money to make money, after all. I have a question. How much money do you want to have by the time you're sixty?"

Before you can answer, Tom rapid-fires a few questions of his own. "Could you tell me more about your house? Where is it? Who's your loan with? When did you buy the property? What was your down payment? What's your interest rate, and what's the term? Fifteen years? Thirty years? Fixed? Variable?"

You don't know where to start. So you answer the last bit. "4.5 percent, thirty-year fixed."

Tom nods with approval. "You know, PMI can be a good thing. It frees up money for other investments. Like our mutual funds."

"Tom's right," Bob says, laying out a pamphlet. "You want to be in the market. Here's our portfolio."

"We've got the top money managers in New York City. Here's their latest market analysis." He places a large, professionally bound book next to the brochure and flips through the tabs. "See, the market analyses are broken out by sector and region." He pushes the tome toward you. "Go ahead, take a look. These guys are good."

Bob continues. "I worked in the New York office for years, as a money manager. I created algorithms for analyzing energy sector stocks."

The market analysis is technical. It's too much to take in. Then Bob says, "Choose which mutual fund you like best, and we'll set you up."

The list is bewildering. You read such names as "All American Industrial Fund" and "Strategic International Markets Fund." Next to each fund are various metrics of performance and composition.

"Could you explain these numbers?" you ask.

"Sure! I'd be happy to! We're in my wheelhouse now! This column is the year-on-year return for someone who invests $50,000 or more, and the other is the return for accounts that drop below $50,000."

"So . . . what exactly are the fees?" you ask.

"Good question!" Bob replies. "For someone investing $50k or more, the fees are just four-tenths of a percent."

That sounds reasonable to you.

Bob adds, "Per quarter."

You think about that for a moment and ask, "So, 1.6 percent per year?"

"Yep. That's the cost of gaining access to stellar funds, managed by our amazing rock stars. Sometimes, you've got to pay a little to get good returns."

You remember your neighbor who retired at forty-five. She'd warned about mutual fund fees. She'd said fees should be less than a half a percent per year. You ask if 1.6 percent is the mutual fund fee.

Tom replies, "Oh no, the mutual fund fees are taken out of the underlying fund at the end of each year. But it's done automatically, so you needn't worry about that. It's all industry standard."

You say, "So, 1.6 percent plus the mutual fund fees?"

But Bob has already moved on, "Did you know we offer refinancing services? We could get you into a 3.5 percent home loan. The right mortgage can get you closer to your savings goals."

"But I don't know what my savings goals are," you object. "Aren't we getting ahead of ourselves? I want to know how to manage my money. We haven't talked about saving for my kids' college funds or retirement."

"Why didn't you tell us you had kids? Sit tight, I'll be right back with our 529 plans!"

You feel like a sheep being led to the slaughter and decide to leave—pronto!

"Oh my," you say. "Look at the time. It's time to get back to work." You exit before Bob returns with more brochures.

What went wrong?

Bob and Tom failed to start with the goal of uncovering your situation, your goals, and your challenges. Instead, they pursued self-serving agendas: to sell you products whether they suited you or not. They selectively heard what they wanted to hear and went straight into selling mode. Tactically they failed, too, rapid-firing questions at you.

No one took notes. That's a cardinal sin in a customer meeting. Note-taking conveys interest. It also ensures an accurate record of the conversation. This was a bad sales job gone horribly wrong. You were smart to escape.

POINTS OF ALIGNMENT

These customer meeting scenarios ranged from useless time wasters to chaotic mayhem. They produced incomplete, biased, and sometimes incorrect customer information. Not meeting at all would have been better.

In the following chapters, you'll learn what it takes to convert such ad hoc sets of behaviors into skillfully orchestrated actions.

Though the scenarios in this chapter were fictional, they were constructed from my own experiences in real meetings. In those occasional moments of mayhem, the team misfires in all directions like untrained children in a soccer match—all piling on the ball and doing their own thing.

In these scenarios, the team's motivations were misaligned and often misguided. Lacking clearly defined common goals, attendees navigated their own courses. Some tried to be genuinely helpful, but their timing was wrong. Others prescribed solutions before diagnosing the full story. Whatever the individual objectives, the team was not working for a common purpose. This led to chaos, miscommunication, and failure to learn what the customer was trying to do.

Second, the mind-sets were all wrong. People were reactionary, defensive, and self-centered. Inadvertently and despite the best of intentions, they stopped customers from sharing.

Customer-facing, tactical skills were lacking as well. For example, people blurted out poorly structured statements, asked loaded questions, talked excessively, and jumped from one subject to another too quickly. That unskilled behavior can completely turn off customers. The teams seemed to lack diplomacy, consideration, and interest.

Last, the roles were not clearly defined. No one took notes, or people spoke too long about pet topics, or others randomly interjected questions whether they applied to the discussion or not. The order and flow bumped about as attendees took control at their whim.

If everyone would have agreed on common goals, mind-sets, skills, and roles, these meetings could have been productive and even enjoyable.

Once a team agrees on these points of alignment, they can uncover highly useful customer information. On such a team, you may find yourself even looking forward to meetings.

CHAPTER SEVEN

Aligning Skills: Questioning

"Management teams aren't good at asking questions. In business school, we train them to be good at giving answers." —Clayton Christensen

THERE ARE SOME basic skills you need in your toolbox to work within a team to align with your customers. These tools will give you the grounding you need to excel in customer interactions and learn the information your team and company need.

The customer aligning techniques I recommend are rooted in what's commonly called "active listening" (AL). Active listening is about asking open-ended, customer-focused, and future-focused questions. Active listening questions (ALQs) provide customers with the freedom to answer honestly and take the conversation in any direction that's important to the customer. And that's precisely where you want the conversation to go.

In this section, we'll review the mechanics of active listening and learn how to craft ALQs. You'll know how to ask questions that inspire thoughtful and truthful answers. When you use these skills with customers, you can't help but project genuine interest. In return, you may be surprised to learn some underlying realities you may never have learned otherwise. You'll have discovered customer insights that matter.

THE ART OF QUESTIONING

When questions are crafted thoughtfully, meetings quickly slip into flow. A seemingly electric connection develops as customers excitedly share ideas.

This chapter covers the basics. Make these skills second nature by practicing them often. Try them with colleagues, over lunch, or at home with the family. Try them at cocktail parties. Observe how the quality of your interactions changes.

You'll want to make these skills habitual. Here's why. In the midst of a conversation with a customer, you want to give your consciousness the freedom to fully focus on the content of what's being said. You don't want to interrupt your thought processes by downshifting into the mechanics of active listening. So practice and make active listening a part of who you are.

Active listening starts with asking the right questions, or active listening questions (ALQs). The following is the recipe for crafting such questions.

ALQs are open-ended.

An open-ended question is one that inspires a thoughtful and thorough answer, free of the influence of suggestion. Open-ended questions typically start with *What? Which? How? Why?* and *Where?* For example:

- What functions would you consider outsourcing?

- What specific actions will you take to achieve your stated goal of sustainability?

- Which protocols will you consider adopting in the next product?

- How might you go about solving that problem you just identified?

- Why are you thinking of (insert some plan the customer just mentioned)?

- Where would you consider moving manufacturing operations to?

Open-ended questions are great in that they prompt the customer to answer in their own terms and to give a complete answer. Contrast this with closed-ended questions that narrow the set of possible answers and lead the witness. Typically closed-ended questions are of the yes/no or multiple choice variety. They are to be avoided.

ALQs are *not* yes/no questions.

The problem with yes/no questions is that they narrow down the set of possible answers to just two one-word answers. They fail to invite further explanation. This is of limited value in customer alignment meetings.

You can recognize many yes/no questions by the words they begin with. These include *Have, Are, Will,* and *Do*. For example:

- Have you ever considered the competing product?

- Are you going to continue using this test program?

- Will you be attending the upcoming trade show in Las Vegas?

- Do you plan to upgrade to the next software build this year?

Answers to Have/Are/Will/Do questions are usually limited to three: Yes, No, and Maybe. These questions tend to discourage elaboration. While a chatty customer may fill in details, others will not. Ask too many yes/no questions and the flow of information dribbles to a stop.

ALQs are *not* multiple-choice questions.

Similar to yes/no questions, multiple-choice questions narrow the set of answers. But they're worse because they lead the customers into answering in a way the questioner desires. This can be intentional or not. Either way, multiple-choice questions are leading questions.

Asking leading questions is contrary to the goal of understanding customer goals and challenges from the customer's perspective. Leading questions may identify some customer goals and challenges, but the answers will be limited to the questioner's perspective.

In court, lawyers are generally not allowed to lead the witness during direct examination. This means they can't ask questions that suggest specific answers, such as multiple-choice questions.

There's a reason for this. Witnesses are put on the stand in a bench trial so that the judge and jury can tease out the truth. The more that a witness tells their story, in their own words, the more these fact finders can judge whether the witness's story is plausible. Furthermore, when the testimony is expressed as original thoughts, it's easier to tell whether the witness is credible. When the witness answers with words put into his or her mouth by a lawyer, it's difficult to tell if the witness is lying. At that point, it's really the lawyer who is testifying, with the witness as their mouthpiece.

And so it is with customer alignment meetings. When we limit the set of possible answers to yes, no, or a list on a menu or otherwise suggest answers, we are influencing the answers. Information gathered in this way is not credible.

Let's consider an example. Imagine you ask, "Will you implement protocol ABC to lower power, lower costs, or reduce the size?" What if the real answer isn't included as one of the options given? What if the customer chose protocol ABC because the ecosystem supporting it was mature and all their engineers were well versed in developing in that ecosystem? Instead of telling you the real reason, they'll probably choose the truest option of those you provided. Not only is this a wrong answer, but it tells you nothing of their motivations.

Instead, ask open-ended questions and let customers come up with their own words. In this example, you might say, "You said you're implementing protocol ABC. What are your reasons for choosing this protocol?" When you ask questions like this, you can trust the customer's answer.

Now, there are times when it's appropriate to ask leading questions. For example, if the customer is elaborating on topics way beyond the scope of the meeting and time is running out, a leading question can bring the conversation back on track. Or if you want quick clarification that you heard correctly, you might ask a yes/no question. These are the exceptions.

In general, try to avoid closed-ended questions, including yes/no questions and multiple-choice questions. You'll find the answers you hear are much more satisfying, useful, and truthful. The answers may spur more questions.

ALQs ask about the future.

Consider this open-ended question: "What protocols do you implement in your product?" I would recommend you change the focus to the future and ask, "What protocols do you plan to implement in your next-generation products?"

Even if you don't know details of the customer's current product, that's okay. The customer will fill in relevant details about present circumstances in support of the answer about future plans. This may feel odd but, trust me, the customer won't skip a beat. By asking about the future, you learn the customer's goals and anticipated challenges. If you start with their current product, you risk getting bogged down in details that don't matter for the purposes of planning products.

ALQs focus on the customer.

If you're responsible for developing "ABC protocol," you have an overwhelming number of decisions to make. You may be tempted to ask the customer how they'd make those decisions in your shoes. You explain some of the trade-offs and design considerations and then pose implementation questions.

How is the customer supposed to answer? You're asking the customer to come into your world of angst, when that's not her natural habitat. What's more, the customer now feels pressure to answer on behalf of all customers in your market and that's a lot of responsibility. You've put the customer in a most uncomfortable position.

As a result, you'll likely hear a watered-down answer such as "Well, I suppose it depends on your customer base. I'd think people would like to have flexibility of option A, but then again they might want the easy-to-use option B. . . ."

Was that answer helpful? No. Why? Because you asked the customer to do your job for you. That's not the customer's role. The customer's role is to share their goals and challenges within the context of *their* future projects. As a result, you heard nothing more than worrisome thoughts that enter your mind when you can't fall asleep at night. You've obtained nothing of use.

A better question would focus on the customer's perspective: "Protocol ABC comes in many shapes and sizes. For your next product, what options do you plan to implement?"

Now the customer can reply freely. There's no pressure as there's no need to speak on behalf of all customers because they are speaking only of their own objectives. This is within the customer's area of expertise and beyond yours. This information is of the most value to you.

"Well, we need one version that is slow and basic. We use it for control commands. We want it to work reliably and take up minimum space. It can operate at kilobytes per second for all I care. The other one will be high performance. We don't plan on using many of the low-power options the spec provides for or any of the data processing. It's just a fat, dumb data pipe. Ideally I'd want two totally separate versions of the protocol that work out of the box. One for control commands, and one for high-speed data."

Now you have a good idea of what the customer is trying to do and you can ask follow-up questions to further your understanding. In fact, now that it's clear you're talking about the customer's specific situation, you have the freedom to ask a few trade-off questions such as "If we offered only this variant of the IP, how would you design around that limitation?" Warning: Don't get carried away with trade-off questions. If the customer starts to feel like you don't care about their plans and you only want to use her to make trade-off decisions, she might grow cold toward you and the team. So ask self-interested questions in moderation as follow-ups to customer-centric questions.

Best practice: Write down ALQs before the customer alignment meeting.

If you craft your core active listening questions ahead of time, you'll be more likely to ask them in a skillful way. Crafting ALQs in advance curtails loaded, rapid-fire, or rambling questions. If you're a subject matter expert, write down a few topic-specific ALQs. Share them with your teammates in the premeeting and ask for suggestions to improve them so that they conform to the rules described in this chapter.

Follow up with Active Listening After Questions (ALAQs).

After you've asked an open-ended, future-looking, and customer-focused question, the customer might answer with an elaborate reply. You're done, right?

Hardly. That was only one answer. An open-ended question often has many answers. In fact, the first answer, even if elaborate, might be worthless. Why? Because it's the knee-jerk response. It's whatever was at the top of the customer's mind. The first answer is usually safe, easy, and obvious. It may not be the critical customer insight that matters.

Never fear. There's a quick way to get to the facts you want to discover. Simply use "active listening after questions" (ALAQs). After receiving the first response to an ALQ, follow it up by asking, "What else?" or "Anything else?" These ALAQs prompt the customer to dig deeper and share more. For example, imagine you asked that ALQ presented above, "For your next product, what options from protocol ABC do you plan to implement?" The customer answers that they need option A because they need to pass a lot of data.

You then ask, "What else?"

The customer says, "Well, we need option two as well, obviously."

Then you ask, "Anything else?" And the customer supplies another answer.

Keep going until the customer says they're done.

Asking follow-up questions gets the customer thinking deeply about the main question you asked, sometimes discovering for the first time many factors they themselves never considered. The lights go on. ALAQs turn your initial question into a productive conversation for everyone. These are when many aha moments arise.

Recall the original question within occasional ALAQs.

Asking "What else?" more than a few times in a row can feel awkward. Also, by then, the customer may have forgotten what the original question was. This is when adding a small reminder of the original question gets the conversation back on track.

For example, instead of asking, "What else?" you might ask, "What other options might you consider using?"

Pepper ALAQs with restatement.

Occasionally, restate what you've heard so far in response to the original ALQ. When you restate what you've heard, you demonstrate that you've been listening and paying attention. The customer may open up and share even more, a natural response when a person feels he's being heard.

Furthermore, restatements encourage customers to clarify and elaborate upon previous answers. More often than not, when customers hear their comments played back, they realize that they've left out critical information. They naturally proceed to fill in the holes. Or if you misstate something (which is totally okay), they'll correct you straightaway. This process, of hearing their words played back, prompts customers to think even more deeply about their answers. At this point, you've gone beyond top-of-the-head responses and into real truths. These are the customer insights that matter.

Here's a tip when restating what you heard. Repeat the very same phrasing the customer used. Don't add insights of your own or try to put the answer in your own words. If you introduce orthogonal thoughts of your own, the customer may argue with you. The thing is the customer can't argue against their own words. More likely, they'll fill in missing information, clarify statements, explain exceptions, or correct the record. That's precisely what you want. Remember, you're on a mission to uncover the whole, nuanced, truthful story from the customer's perspective. Getting into arguments about some throwaway comment of yours will lead you off course.

Active listening after question restatement is one of the most powerful questioning techniques in this book. To use it requires that you start with well-crafted active listening questions. It requires intention, practice, and verbatim note-taking. Having notes that reflect what the customer just said is an invaluable tool when you're restating what the customer, well, just said. Don't wing it. Don't go from memory. As you'll learn later, our memories are selective, leaky, and untrustworthy. For the moment, though, just know that if you take verbatim notes, you'll quickly become a master at restating what you just heard. Get ready for the firehose of meaningful customer information to come at you.

You're not done with an ALQ/ALAQ series of questioning until the customer says you're done.

You may find that you've asked "What else?" and "Anything else?" a dozen times. If the customer is still answering, by golly, keep asking those active listening after questions! Keep using restatement and reprompting with the original active listening question. The entire team sticks with this line of questioning until the customer says they have nothing to add. It can take a while. That's why you should . . .

Allow plenty of time for each ALQ.

Done right, each active listening question will take anywhere from five to thirty minutes. That's how much time the customer might need to get out the full answer. The amount of time will depend on the customer, the topic, and the degree to which your colleagues work with you to extract a full answer. Make that time count by preparing your questions in advance. Only ask questions that are important enough to take up a significant portion of the meeting. If the answer isn't worth spending thirty minutes on, then don't ask the question or at least save it for later, if there's time.

The whole team needs to be in on it.

If even a single person on the aligning team is unaware of how active listening questions and active listening after questions work, they could derail the conversation before the full answer has been heard. They might ask questions that veer the customer off course from answering the original ALQ or they might ask a totally unrelated question. ALQ/ALAQ only works when everyone is in on it. When they are, teammates can take turns restating and asking ALAQs. Make sure the entire team knows what's going on.

That's it! Those are the core fundamentals of asking ALQs. We'll build upon these throughout the book. Become familiar with the concepts. Practice them often, both in and outside of the customer alignment meetings.

LISTENING WITHOUT OVERCOMMITTING

Aligning entails listening to what customers say they want but not necessarily doing what they say. While you are asking carefully crafted active listening questions, it's imperative to keep this in mind. Attentively gather information from them, but be careful in how you implement any feedback.

Aligning entails kindly listening to what customers say they want and then not building the product they ask for.

Customers have all sorts of ideas of what they want you to create for them. They may feel strongly that they need a speedy widget with hovering capabilities. Or they may say they require an FPGA that closes timing at 1GHz on a 1024-bit data path with hundreds of 50Gbps transceivers and an enormous amount of random access memory—all while burning less power than a high-efficiency light bulb. (By the time this book is finished, who knows? That all may be possible!) A business-to-business (B2B) client may not be well versed in database architecture, and yet they may ask you to develop a complex app to interact with their customer relationship management system.

Why don't you go and do what the customer says they want? Well, for one thing, it may be impossible to build. Or it may be extremely expensive to implement. Or in the case of the B2B app, it may violate all kinds of privacy contracts that are in place with the end customers.

Down this fool's path, you could commit a tremendous amount of time, resources, and materials only to deliver a product that the customer cannot afford. The reason to listen and then shelve customer product implementation recommendations is because your business practices are *your* area of expertise, not the customer's.

- Don't ask customers for product specifications because these *are not* customer areas of expertise.

- Do discover customer goals and challenges because these *are* customer areas of expertise.

Let me share an example of how this shouldn't go. This is from Rob Sturgill, a former colleague from Altera, after he brought on a new engineer to provide customer support:

"Within weeks, my new employee returned from a set of meetings with a laundry list of features the customer 'absolutely needed'—a huge warning flag. I'd found that the biggest hurdle to successful customer negotiation was the ability to distinguish customer wants from needs and find a way to navigate toward mutually beneficial (win-win) solutions."

When Rob later attended meetings along with new employees, he witnessed them turning into yes-men, blindly recording every request the customer made. He said, "As quickly as a customer would utter their needs, these colleagues would embark upon a crusade to deliver that request. They thought the customer was always right. No, the customer is not always right."

If you're not going to implement customer suggestions, why even consult with them? Because your expertise ends where theirs begins. You may know how to specify or build a widget, but customers are the ultimate experts in what they want to do with such a widget. They're intimately aware of their current experience with the tools available to them today. They can painstakingly describe the flurry of challenges they've encountered. Most important, they can tell you, better than any market expert, just what they are trying to achieve in the future. When aligning, uncover the topics in which customers are the experts: their own goals and challenges. You can fill in the rest.

Heed the lesson of Homer.

On occasion, I've heard colleagues ask customers something like "So what do you want us to build for you?" Immediately, my mind conjures up an image of "the Homer."

In episode fifteen, season two, of *The Simpsons*, titled "Oh Brother, Where Art Thou?", Homer Simpson discovers he has a half-brother, Herb. Herb owns a Detroit car company and decides that Homer perfectly encapsulates his target customer: "the everyday man."

Herb is sick and tired of turning out tired derivatives of the same car over and over. He introduces Homer to his design team and tells them to come up with a car for the everyday man.

The design lead asks Homer, "So, uh, what kind of car would you like, Mr. Simpson?" Homer knows nothing of onboard computers, nor what Homer calls rack-and-peanut steering. Realizing Homer's ineptness, the design team bulldozes ahead, totally ignoring Homer's input. Exasperated, Herb puts Homer in charge, telling the designers to build exactly what Homer asks for. *Doh!*

The car they produce is a hideous mess. With a bubble cabin, enormous tail fins, and a sticker price of $140,000 (in 2018 dollars), "The Homer" is far too expensive for the everyday man, not to mention the fact that it's a repulsive monstrosity.

The design team failed to ask Homer about how he'd use the car. They could have asked where he drives, what image he wants to project, and whether he eats or drinks in the car. They presumed to know what Homer wanted and failed to ask any open-ended, Homer-focused questions.

When Homer was put in charge, the team blindly designed exactly what he specified, even though he clearly had no idea what he was asking for. Homer had no expertise in car design, nor in manufacturing. Yet they implemented his product designs. The design team should have probed further. By taking Homer literally, the team failed to uncover why he wanted each item. For example, when Homer said he wanted a bubble hood, perhaps what he was really asking for was better visibility in all directions. When he said he wanted giant tail fins, perhaps he was yearning for classic but edgy styling. Okay, maybe I'm overanalyzing a cartoon. Nevertheless, if you're in product development, I urge you to heed Homer's cautionary tale.

For any topic, always remember that the customer is the expert on *their needs*. Don't ask to hear what you know or fish for confirmation of what you suspect. Instead, put aside what you know and ask questions that probe customers for what they are experts in: their road map, their goals, and their challenges. Begin with uncovering and be sure to record the answers carefully. Then be even more careful in how you treat any action items gleaned from the discussion.

ACTION ITEMS (WHEN YOU CAN'T AVOID THEM)

By and large, customer alignment meetings aren't the place to commit to action items. Action items are any specific tasks that someone commits to completing sometime soon after a meeting. An action item could be a promise to send an e-mail confirming a piece of information that was shared. Or an action item could be a promise to include a specific functionality in a future product.

The problem with signing up for laundry lists of action items is that they distract from the true purpose of CA meetings: to uncover customer goals and challenges for the future.

If you do take on an action item, you are 100 percent responsible for it from start to finish. You write it down yourself and you follow up on it personally (copying the host on all e-mails with the customer). If someone volunteers for an action item during a CA meeting, they need to know to rely only upon themselves to remember to close it out.

That said, the official notetaker for a meeting session (aka scribe) *should* record action items too—mainly to ensure accurate records are kept. Scribes are not responsible for tracking, nor for closing, action items.

For anyone writing down an action item that is their responsibility, a good practice is to mark these passages with some sort of bold symbol. For example, you could write "AR," which is short for action request, and then circle the acronym a few times to call attention to that line.

Allowing action items to go unrecorded leads to verbal commitments going unaddressed. Every unaddressed commitment strains the relationship with the customer. It's better not to set expectations than to commit to some action and fail to follow through. Failures like these degrade the confidence the customer has in you, in your team, and in your company.

Don't be a yes-man unless you intend to close the deal yourself.

A senior director, new to our company, popped into a meeting I was hosting. He'd never attended any training sessions but sat through about three hours of the meeting nonetheless. Every so often, he'd interrupt the customer midsentence and say, "We'll find that out for you" or "We'll follow up on that." He racked up at least a dozen action items through the course of the meeting.

At the break, I asked when we could expect him to follow up. He looked at me with a confused expression and said, "You should ask the team. They'll handle it." This person didn't even know all the names of the people on our aligning team, and he expected them to handle all his willy-nilly action items. I let him know that he—and he alone—was responsible for closing out the list of actions he'd signed up for.

Fortunately, a session scribe had recorded every item and was able to send him the full list by the end of the day.

Unfortunately, this senior director did nothing. Weeks later, the salesperson on the account discovered that not a single action had been closed. He was irate. After that meeting, I refused to allow this yes-man into meetings with his customers.

If you want to be a respected member of the aligning team or simply wish to get along with your coworkers, don't assume others will pick up action items you sign up for. If you're not willing to follow up yourself, then don't volunteer.

Be Teflon.

The best policy is to resist taking action items. Usually action items have to do with current-day issues. However, the purpose of customer alignment meetings is to talk about futures. Such a discussion should not result in a long list of pending items to follow up on. Sure, customers may mention all manner of ideas and actions they'd like your company to take on. Rather than take an action to see whether an idea is possible, use the comment as a starting point to further understand the customer's goals and challenges. Instead of saying, "I'll look into that idea and get back to you," turn the request around and ask, "What obstacles are you trying to overcome by seeking this particular solution?" Get them talking about their goals and challenges, not what they think should be your goals.

Yes, I'm telling you to deflect action items. I'll say it again because everyone on the team needs to understand: in a CA meeting, you should err on the side of not picking up action items. Instead, double down on learning why the customer is making such requests. If, in the end, you sign up to take some action, make sure that you close it out in a timely manner.

Note it, but don't commit to it.

Here's what I suggest instead: even if you want to follow up on some item the customer raises, quietly note the issue for yourself without saying anything about following up on it later. Then, on your own time, research the answer. If it seems appropriate at that point, get back to the customer independently. It's better to come through with information having set no expectations than to do the opposite: fail to deliver having promised to get back to her or him.

You may have every intention during the customer alignment meeting of following up. You may find yourself sitting excitedly with your arm raised high in the air, like Horshack on *Welcome Back Kotter*, saying, "*Ooh ooh ooh*, me!" Nope. Curb your enthusiasm. In the real world, after the meeting, you'll likely return to your desk where an overwhelming amount of work is waiting for you. In the to-do list triage process, the action item that so excited you in the CA meeting might slip away unaddressed. That's okay if you haven't set any expectations. It's unacceptable if you've made a commitment.

Occasionally, action items are okay.

That being said, sometimes taking on an action item is entirely appropriate. For example, you might not be certain that an important schedule is still on track. If timing is critical to the customer, by all means go back and confirm the schedule and let the customer know your findings as soon as possible. Use your best judgment.

The main thing is this: if you do take on an action item in a customer alignment meeting, it is your responsibility to record the action and see to its closure. Because your task will be in the meeting notes, the customer will possess a written document attesting to the fact that you owe them information. It's your responsibility— and yours alone—to deliver a response.

CHAPTER EIGHT

The Art of Questioning, Continued

"The advanced level is mastery of the basics." —Ray Mancini

You now know how to ask questions, use restatement to elicit answers that matter, and refrain from committing to too much follow-up. Now it's time to fine-tune your skills further. Remember, active listening questions are open-ended, future-oriented, and customer-focused. That's great. But what happens after you ask the question? Short answer: Shut up and listen. Long answer: Be quiet and patient enough to receive the response and then use the special active listening after questions (ALAQs) introduced in the previous chapter (e.g., "What else?") to ensure you get a full answer. In this chapter, we'll further explore how to put these and other techniques to effective use.

Get comfortable with silence.

There often comes a time during a questioning session when the customer is deep in thought, considering how to answer. The silence can feel awkward. But it's a good thing! Don't ruin it by commandeering the conversation. Don't jump in with a list of options the customer might choose from. Remember that offering multiple-choice answers can be worse than simply asking a yes/no question. In other words, get comfortable with silence.

If the customer looks up at the ceiling or contorts his facial features in some way, he's in deep thought. Give him as much time as needed. You may feel like you're putting the customer on the spot. You aren't. Shut up and let the customer think. In fact, when you witness the customer thinking deeply, revel in it. This is precisely why you invited him to the customer alignment meeting!

You're not done until *the customer* says you're done.

You have lots of questions. You know how to craft an active listening question and the follow-up active listening after questions. When do you stop? We covered this briefly before, but it's critical that everyone on the team know the answer. You are only done with an ALQ/ALAQ series when the customer says so.

Let's attend an imaginary meeting and put our questioning skills to the test.

The team understands that the objective is to uncover customer goals and challenges. The meeting won't be over until all customer goals and challenges have been uncovered.

Imagine you've asked a question, something like "What goals will you establish for your next-generation Widget 3000?"

The customer answers, "We want to reduce the form factor by 30 percent."

Do you stop there? Heck, no. That was only one goal. It may not be the most important answer. In fact, it may not be the real answer. To get the real answer, you've got to double down.

You ask, "What else?"

The customer replies, "We also want to reduce power consumption by 20 percent. By reducing the form factor, we concentrate the heat. They don't make heat sinks big enough. Besides, increasing the size of the heat sink would be counter to our goal of reducing size and weight. So we've calculated we need to draw 20 percent less power."

You scribble the answer in your notebook, as does the session scribe. You think, *Wow, that was solid info.* Do you stop there? No. Why? Because the customer hasn't told you they're done.

You ask another ALAQ: "Any other goals?"

After considering your question for a moment, the customer replies, "Well, yeah. We're going after a new market with this product. We aren't 100 percent sure that the functionality is exactly what they'll want. Even as we're optimizing for low power, we need to maintain some ability to do in-system upgrades so that we can roll out functionality as we determine it's needed."

You hadn't seen that coming. As you record the answer in the customer's words, you're dying to ask for more details about how they envision implementing this, as this is precisely the technology you're working on.

You're about to jump down that rabbit hole when a teammate restates what the team has heard so far: "Okay, so we've heard footprint reduction of 30 percent. Power reduction of 20 percent to reduce heat to manageable levels and in-system upgrades in shipped products. What other goals have you established for your next-generation Widget 3000?"

Wow, that teammate of yours executed that ALAQ to perfection. The restatement conveyed what had been heard and reminded the customer of the original question, keeping the customer on track.

The customer is quiet, and his eyes roam the walls of the room. You see a colleague, a director from the software engineering department, squirming in his chair. *Uh-oh*, you think, *he's about to talk.* That's the worst thing that can happen now. You want the customer digging deep, thinking up other goals. The last thing you need is someone on your team disrupting the customer's deep consideration. This is customer gold territory; you'll be damned if anyone disrupts it. You make eye contact with your squiggly teammate and very slightly shake your head. He sits on his hands as if that'll stop him from saying anything. *Well, at least he got the message,* you think. So you nod affirmation, all while your eyelids lower in a show of benevolent approval.

Interminable seconds pass. More colleagues squirm as the customer distorts a puckering mouth to the side and squints. At long last, the customer says, "I think the other goals are the same as all our products: get to market as fast as possible; craft highly stylized chassis that are clean, simple, and modern; and make the supporting software as simple and user-friendly as possible. But all those goals are beyond my area of responsibility."

Awesome answer, you think as you write down his words into your notebook. Are you done yet? No. The customer hasn't told you you're done. As awkward as it feels, you double down again.

"Any other goals?" you ask.

"Actually," the customer says, "yeah, there is another goal. It's more of an internal operational goal, but as our products grow in complexity, it's becoming important. We need systems and processes that allow us to collaborate more efficiently. In the past, our teams haven't worked well together. I'd never thought about that as a goal—working across teams effectively—but to be honest it's critical for meeting our ever tightening schedules and what management calls 'hairy audacious goals.'"

Wow, that was cool. You want to take a bow. Your squirmy colleague is beaming. You can tell he's about to talk. Uh-oh, though. That'd be bad, because you're still not done. The customer just served up another goal, a big, hairy, audacious goal, but he didn't say he was done. You've gotta keep at it. So you say, "That's awesome. Any other goals?"

The customer thinks for all two seconds and says, "Nope, that's it. Those are all the goals we have for the Widget 3000."

There it is. There's your end stop. Now you're done. Now you can move on to the next active listening question that you'd written down before the meeting or, alternatively, delve into any of the responses the customer just volunteered; you could ask about in-system upgrades or cross-departmental collaboration, for example. The customer said that he was finished with your original question and now you have the clearance to move on. Only the customer has the right, in a customer alignment meeting, to indicate that a particular line of questioning is over.

Until you hear the customer say something to the effect of "Yeah, that's all" or "Nope, that's it," your job is to keep asking ALAQs until you've heard every answer.

You're thinking about all this when the customer interrupts your thoughts. "Hey, thanks. You really forced me to think that through. I hadn't thought much about how important the operational intergroup dynamics were until now. I think I'll call that out as an area to plan for in upcoming projects. Maybe we can work with you to make improvements."

Now you know precisely how important that reporting feature is to this customer. And so does squirmy guy from software engineering—the same guy who developed that very feature; the same guy who was at a loss for defending it when his department head put it on the chopping block the other day. You look over to your colleague and see he's still beaming. Now he has a case for saving the feature he developed. And now the uncovering team has a chance to explore further details with the customer directly in the alignment meeting.

When one person asks a question, the team asks a question.

In this example, your colleague jumped in and asked an appropriate follow-up question to your original question, restating the customer's answers and then asking, "What other goals have you established for your next-generation Widget 3000?" That's what professional uncovering looks like. Every person in the room understands that when an ALQ is asked, it is the job of the team to stay on that question until they get a full and complete answer.

This is why it's so important that every single attendee take the same training. All it takes is one person who doesn't comprehend her role to take the meeting down rabbit holes. This leads to not hearing the full story. Do enough of this and you lose the connection, you lose the flow. And you may fail to uncover critical information.

Statements are not questions.

On occasion I've encountered attendees who feel uncomfortable asking direct questions. I've been told that it feels too forward, as if they're putting the customer on the spot. News flash: you're not putting the customer on the spot! They are in the customer alignment meeting in order to answer your questions. Don't equivocate, simply ask your well-crafted active listening questions.

For example, a shy teammate might want to ask, "What reasons do you have for picking ABC protocol?" In an effort to avoid confrontation, they might instead state, "Customers seem to have lots of different reasons for picking ABC protocol."

While an answer might be expected, instead all that's received is a blank stare. Why? Because this person didn't ask a question; they made a statement.

Don't ask multiple-choice questions.

Another common hedge is to ask a question and immediately ramble off a list of possible answers, as if the customer is taking a multiple-choice test. This often happens when the questioner is uncomfortable with silence. They mistake a customer's silence as discomfort. Then they bail out the quiet customer with a list of possible answers.

As we've already learned, multiple-choice questions are leading questions and leading questions introduce bias; they influence the customer. That's not good when you're trying to tease out the real truth.

Ask one question at a time.

You may have lots of questions and may be eager to learn the answers. After waiting patiently for your turn to ask questions, you may feel a need to get them all on the table before the meeting moves on to another subject. This can lead to rapid-fire questions, where you ask multiple questions all at once.

This is precisely what happened to Bob, the financial planner, featured in Chapter Six: "How Not to Align." Poor Bob was so keen on getting all his questions out that he asked a dizzying number of questions in rapid-fire succession.

Bob asked, "Could you tell me more about your house? Where is it? Who's your lender? When did you buy the property? What was your down payment? What's your interest rate, and what's the term? Fifteen years? Twenty years? Thirty years? Fixed or variable?"

Hoo-boy. What a fire hose! The rapid firing of multiple questions is not only inconsiderate but nearly impossible to answer.

Besides being annoyed, when a customer hears a long list of rapid-fire questions, she tends to only remember the final one or two. So she answers those. There's no hope for the customer to answer all of them. Turn off the fire hose, and instead ask one question at a time and listen for the full answer before moving on.

Ask the question you actually want to ask.

If you want to better understand the factors that are considered when customers choose devices for a particular function, then ask the customer a question that will get him thinking about what goes into device selection. If you were in a meeting, asking questions off the top of your head, you might ask, "Why do you select one device over another?"

That's not an awful question, but it's too vague and doesn't make the customer think about a concrete example. He'll have a hard time getting into details when your question feels so high level. Instead, ask, "What factors do you consider when you evaluate various device options for this particular function?"

Now you've given the customer something concrete to focus on and you've asked the question you actually want to ask. Also, by asking for "factors," you tee up active listening after questions such as "What other factors . . . ?" Again, if you craft the question in advance, you can ensure that it is open-ended, future-focused, and customer-centric.

Don't be afraid to ask "What did you mean?"

If it's unclear what the customer meant by something, for goodness' sake, ask what was meant. Try to restate exactly what was said as part of the question, to provide a springboard for elaboration and provide an opportunity for clarification if you got something wrong.

Beware the rabbit hole.

Imagine that topic A is being discussed. One person comments and, in doing so broaches topic B. Another person elaborates on topic B with gusto, whether or not everyone is done discussing topic A. Now the discussion is on B, and the team fails to return to topic A. They move on to topic C and then D.

Conversations like these are natural. It's how we chat at a party or with friends over lunch. However, in a business meeting, where the goal is to fully discuss topic A, this very human habit of following one diversion after another will leave everyone dissatisfied.

Sticking with the topic takes discipline and conscious intent. If there's even one person who has not learned how to ask active listening questions, you are very likely to get diverted down rabbit holes. All it takes is for the customer to answer with a comment that piques an attendee's curiosity. And bam! You're off topic. Make sure everyone on your team knows how to listen for the customer signal that topic A has been answered and discussed in full before moving on.

Avoid asking questions that start with "Out of curiosity."

Earlier, I recommended that every customer alignment meeting start with a reminder for everyone to let their curiosity drive their questions. This makes sense when the questions are earnest and within the realm of the current topic. However, sometimes questions that start with "I'm just curious" or "Out of curiosity" come off badly. They feel like the questions are afterthoughts, as if the questioner doesn't really care what the answer is or is somehow failing to value the customer's time. We'll discuss this further in chapter seventeen on common meeting traps.

Drop a Cunningham bomb.

If you really want to know what the customer thinks about something and it seems they aren't telling you the full story, then pull out your nukes. It's time to drop a Cunningham bomb.

Cunningham's Law, named after the "father of wikis," states that "the best way to get the right answer . . . is not to ask a question, it's to state the wrong answer." In a customer meeting, this means taking one for the team and making yourself look like a complete moron. It's where you make an assertion that's dead wrong. The customer won't only correct the statement but will likely fill in background information. He might realize that not everyone in the room shares his knowledge base and so will start sharing his knowledge.

This is an advanced strategy that requires teamwork. Every person on the aligning team must know how to handle a Cunningham bomb: step way back and let it drop unimpeded on the customer. An unaware team member might step in to answer, detonating the nuke in its silo. Remember the executive in one of the "How Not to Align" stories? He would not have tolerated a Cunningham bomb for an instant and would have jumped in to bail out the customer immediately.

When someone drops the Cunningham bomb, pay close attention to the customer reaction. The information the customer gives should be captured as well as possible.

A good example of a Cunningham bomb in action is a story a friend of mine told me about Gary, a sales guy he worked with. Everyone agreed Gary was both irritating and annoying. At first, my friend couldn't stand visiting customers with him because Gary would say outrageously idiotic things in meetings. Then one day, my friend realized that Gary did this on purpose. He found that Gary's idiotic assertions got the customers talking; they felt an obligation to correct him. In one meeting, the customers were unwilling to divulge exactly which product they were interested in. The different devices came in various sizes, characterized by the number of "gates." Gates are like on/off switches and are used in logical circuits. The more gates one has, the more complex a design one can implement.

In previous meetings, the customers had been asking for price quotes for all the various devices but were unwilling to divulge exactly which device they were interested in. In a subsequent meeting, Gary and my friend needed to know exactly what device the customer was interested in, mainly so they could convey the specific requirements to engineering. But the customer continued being obtuse.

So five minutes into the conversation Gary says, "We understand your design is 880,000 gates and will grow by up to 6 percent within a year."

With that "ball rolling across the table," as my friend put it, a junior engineer from the customer company physically jumped up in protest. "No, no, no, you don't understand. It'll be a million gates, and we'll reduce it over time." My friend dutifully wrote down the information. From there, they were able to carry out an informative discussion as they focused in on the details of this specific scenario.

Mind you, deploying this technique can come at a cost because the person who drops the Cunningham bomb will look like a complete idiot. One mitigating tactic is to establish your credibility with the customer well in advance of dropping the Cunningham bomb. Then, when the customer corrects you, it may even feed their ego to have corrected an expert.

As Gary's colleague noted, "You've got to be comfortable trading your dignity for a little bit of raw information." Just make sure that raw information is worth it.

Remember, this is an advanced technique and should only be attempted by teams of professionals who know how to execute this tactic together. Make sure everyone in the room is comfortable with seemingly stupid (but actually strategic) questions and that every member of the team understands it is never their place to correct a colleague's comments.

And don't even think about dropping a Cunningham bomb when anyone who keeps answering for the visiting company is in the room, like our dear senior director in chapter seven. If someone like that isn't in on the plan, she'll not only answer on the customer's behalf but may go positively apoplectic if you ask questions of the Cunningham variety.

Make sure everyone is working together to ensure your Cunningham bombs result in spectacular success.

Ask trade-off questions.

If you want to know what the customer thinks about a topic he hasn't broached, be careful. Take care to ask about what he cares about, not pet topics of yours. To explore this space, consider asking trade-off questions to understand how much he cares about the subject on your mind.

For example, imagine the customer said he wants faster performance and hasn't said a word about power. However, you and your colleagues are keen to understand customer power requirements. In this case, you might ask, "If we built two products, one with 20 percent faster performance for the same power as you have now and the other with the same performance but 20 percent less total power consumption, which would you prefer?" In this way, the topic you care about is put in trade-off context with a topic your customer cares about. The customer can feel free to think rationally without worrying about sending unintended messages.

Keep in mind that trade-off questions are self-centered, multiple-choice questions. You're supplying answers to choose from. While these questions usually are to be avoided, they can be appropriate sometimes. As long as you don't lead with trade-off questions and you use them sparingly, they are fine to ask as follow-up questions.

When you ask trade-off questions you learn what one of my colleagues called "the customer's indifference curve." In other words, you learn what they care about and to what degree. Your customer may have surprised you by answering your power/performance question by saying they'd take the lower power option, given the choice. This is a perfect opportunity to now ask an active listening question on power. For example, you may ask, "What factors are driving your decision to take 20 percent less power over 20 percent more performance?" This may kick off a ten-minute discussion on the very topic you care about.

After asking trade-off questions, you'll have a better idea of what they're willing to pay a little more for and what they're unwilling to pay anything for. Again, be sure not to lead with trade-off questions because they are self-centered and can start you off on the wrong foot. Similarly, use Cunningham questions sparingly and use them well after you've developed rapport and credibility.

Ask active listening questions that get SMART answers.

Management trainers often teach the practice of setting SMART goals for employees: S = Specific, M = Measurable, A = Attainable, R = Relevant, T = Timely. Developed by George T. Doran and based on Peter Drucker's management by objectives system, SMART goals emphasizes defining goals within a team so that objectives and strategies are clear.

When you're trying to learn your customer's goals, borrow the SMART acronym to craft your questions. Try to learn as many of these five attributes as you can within reason. If the customer can't or won't answer, leave it.

Specific and Measurable: The more you have specific and measurable data points, the better you'll be able to transform the customer's story into actionable product developments at a later time. To get a specific and measurable answer, start your active listening question with the word *what*. For example, you could ask, "What specific criteria would your product have to deliver in order for your market to embrace it?" Be sure to follow up with the active listening after questions until they've provided an entire list. At that point, go back and ask if you can get some specific numbers if you feel the answers were too vague.

Attainable: In the context of a customer alignment meeting, "attainable" describes the gap between what the customer's currently available options provide and how the desired options would improve on what they have now.

Relevant: After discovering a number of goals and challenges on the customer's plate, you can ask them trade-off questions to assess the relevance. In other words, the relative priorities your customer cares about. For example, you might ask, "If you could choose only three of the ten features you listed, which would those be?" The answer you obtain should reveal the relative importance of various needs.

Timely: Note the time frame in which a new product capability would be useful to the customer or, conversely, when it will no longer be valued.

Use the SMART acronym both when crafting your ALQs and in the second half of the meeting, to make sure you fully understood the information uncovered in the first half.

When you are crafting your ALQs, the first question should always be future-focused, open-ended, and customer-centric. Once the customer has finished answering, you may find that you've already heard the attainable piece. At this point, ask clarifying questions to fill in more SMART details. You might ask, "What specific accounts will you be focusing on over the next five years?" Then ask, "What factors are driving the need for the new IT (information technology) infrastructure you plan to adopt?" If, at this point, you still haven't covered all the SMART attributes, you could say, "You stated you will be focusing on accounts in the autonomous driving sector. I'd like to understand what changes that pivot in focus will mean for your organization, in terms of staffing and IT."

Take care, however. You don't want to pester your clients. Ideally, the answers your customers provide when asked about goals and challenges will likely include many SMART attributes. If you get three of five, you're doing well.

Also be careful that you keep your eye on the right ball. You want to stay focused on describing what your customer is trying to achieve. In the process of collecting SMART answers, however, it's easy to slip into focusing on issues from your own project management perspective, not from the customer's. Remember, a customer alignment meeting isn't about translating customer requirements into actionable product specifications. It's about understanding customer goals and challenges.

Prepare questions in advance of the customer alignment meeting.

The aligning team should craft or review their main active listening questions together in a premeeting. If the team writes down the questions exactly as they intend to ask them, they will be likely to ask ALQs that allow the customer to give complete answers.

Having worked together to craft the questions, they'll be patient as one question is answered at a time. They'll be less likely to jump to the next question prematurely and less likely to ask suboptimal questions. The key is preparation.

That said, you needn't write down every single question in advance. The conversation could go in an unexpected direction. If this leads to uncovering surprising customer goals and challenges, you'll want to ask ALQs to delve further. Obviously you can't possibly predict every question to ask in advance. However, if you've practiced writing ALQs with the team, you'll be better positioned to craft ALQs on the fly as needed.

As you gain experience, I encourage you to continue crafting your main ALQs in the premeeting. But don't let those limit you. You can ask other questions too. The more you prepare and practice, the better you'll become at asking ALQs in real time.

QUICK 'N' DIRTY ALQ CRAFTING DECISION TREE

Use this decision tree to craft your active listening questions. Write out your ALQ and then proceed down the tree. When you see an *X*, go back and rephrase your question. When you see an arrow, keep trucking.

1. Does the ALQ focus on your interests or does it ask what the customer cares about?

   Is about you   X (rephrase)

   Is about the customer $\longrightarrow$ (keep trucking)

2. Is the ALQ a yes/no, multiple-choice, or open-ended question?

   Yes/No   X (rephrase)

   Multiple-choice   X (rephrase)

   Open-ended $\longrightarrow$ (keep trucking)

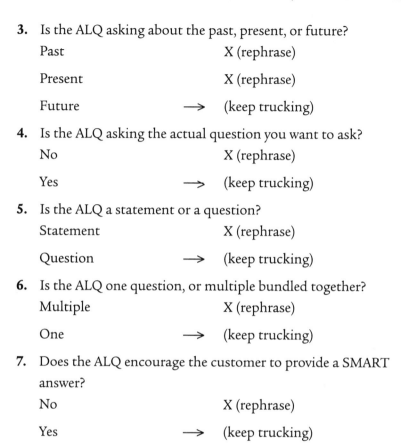

3. Is the ALQ asking about the past, present, or future?

Past   X (rephrase)

Present   X (rephrase)

Future   ⟶   (keep trucking)

4. Is the ALQ asking the actual question you want to ask?

No   X (rephrase)

Yes   ⟶   (keep trucking)

5. Is the ALQ a statement or a question?

Statement   X (rephrase)

Question   ⟶   (keep trucking)

6. Is the ALQ one question, or multiple bundled together?

Multiple   X (rephrase)

One   ⟶   (keep trucking)

7. Does the ALQ encourage the customer to provide a SMART answer?

No   X (rephrase)

Yes   ⟶   (keep trucking)

If you've arrived here, your question is an ALQ. Most of the questions you ask in a customer alignment meeting should be ALQs. Some questions toward the end of each session can be trade-off questions, or clarifying questions to make sure you heard correctly. The more ALQs you ask, the more information you'll learn about the customer's goals and challenges. And that's what you're in the meeting to learn.

CHAPTER NINE

Aligning Skills: Listening

"We have two ears and one mouth so that we can listen twice as much as we speak."
—Epictetus, Greek Stoic philosopher (AD 55–AD 135)

A T THIS POINT you know how to ask questions that get the customer talking. Now it's time to learn how to listen to the answers. Recall that these interview techniques are based on *active listening*. The majority of your time should be spent listening and writing down what you hear. When you feel like chatting during a customer meeting, I implore you to recall the words of the Greek philosopher Epictetus: "We have two ears and one mouth so that we can listen twice as much as we speak."

I'd go so far as to imagine we have four ears and listen in that proportion.

This listening business may sound passive, but I assure you it's not. In this section, we'll focus on how to train your brain to actively tune in to the customer's story, mute your internal monologue, and get comfortable with silence. We'll expand on ways to cultivate curiosity. You'll minimize distractions, both internal and external, and tune in to nonverbal cues.

Sure, you'll talk a little. You'll ask active listening questions and use restatement to check for understanding. However, your chatter will occupy a maximum of 10 to 20 percent of the conversation. The rest of the time, you'll write and listen actively.

This may seem easy but, believe me, it takes practice. We humans, by nature, tune in to our own storylines, filter what we hear, and grow anxious when presented with silence. When we're tasked with *active listening*, we're outside of our comfort zones. Lacking proper tools, we often fall on old habits to regain comfort. So what you need to do is embrace discomfort and stay with it, so you can hear the full story. Here's how.

1. Get comfortable with silence.

2. Minimize distractions, both external and internal.

3. Get comfortable with discomfort.

4. Pay attention to nonverbal cues.

Get comfortable with silence.

We've already touched on the subject of being comfortable with silence, but it's such a critical skill, it's worth discussing further. Let's start by looking into the mind-set of a detective, by hearing what a real detective has to say on the topic.

In a presentation to first-year law students at Regent University, Detective George Bruch of the Virginia Beach Police Department discussed how he used the fear of silence to get suspects to talk or confess. Here's what he said: "I just sit there and wait for them to start talking, because they will. They want to talk. People want to communicate. They hate silence. That's why when people speak you hear *ah* and *uh* . . . because they need to fill that void with something. People hate silence."

Detective Bruch knows what he's talking about. His comfort with silence allows him to wait as long as it takes, whether it's seconds or minutes. He knows that his patience will pay off. He knows that his silence makes the suspect uncomfortable. With that discomfort, the suspect eventually fills in the void with talking. One of the most powerful uncovering tools is being comfortable with silence.

To be fair, a customer meeting isn't a high-stakes criminal interrogation. If it feels that way, then you're doing it wrong. The point here is this natural disposition, this discomfort with silence, is very real and very human. If you don't recognize this and learn how to overcome it, you may never hear the full story from your customer. Why? Because if you fill the silence with your own dialogue, you are denying the customer time and space to think deeply about how to answer your questions and get out the full story. Instead, you'll likely limit yourself to hearing superficial answers that do not constitute the whole story or, worse, you just hear yourself talk. You may as well not have the meeting if you can't give the customer the time needed to formulate full answers.

Remember the active listening questions you've written down? They are open-ended, customer-centric, and future-focused. It may be that this is the first time the customer is truly considering your question. Your job is to let the customer take as much time as necessary. Don't disrupt this process by filling the silence, even if he's looking around and seems uncomfortable. Let him think.

If you still can't bear silence, I suggest you come up with ways to endure it. Here are some tactics that can help you get comfortable with silence. I've listed quite a few ideas here because, yes, keeping your mouth shut is *that* important.

- Sit on your hands. I'm not sure what's going on with this one psychologically. Perhaps by suppressing gesturing, it makes a gesturing talker less likely to speak. In any case, it seems to work for some people. If you tend to gesture when you talk, you may find it works for you.

- Cover your mouth with a hand. Place your elbow on the table and rest your chin in the cupped palm of your hand as the fingers rest on your lips, reminding them not to move.

- Project an encouraging smile toward the customer, communicating patience and interest. It's an expression that says, "Take all the time you need. This information is supremely important and not to be rushed."

- Remind yourself that these are the moments of striking customer gold. This is what the team strives for. Savor every passing second. Tell yourself, if it's uncomfortable, it's working.

- Silently repeat the ALQ that was asked, that the customer is currently pondering. This will reinforce the context of the customer's answer when an answer is voiced.

- Silently count backward from ten to one. Keep going until the customer answers.

- Doodle in your notebook.

- Silently count to twenty in a foreign language.

Whatever you need to do to get comfortable with silence, do it. Make sure everyone else on the team does the same. All it takes is one person breaking the silence to bungle the moment.

Minimize internal distractions.

A very real challenge lies in minimizing distractions and staying focused. The reason is this: Our brains are discursive by nature. When we hear a familiar topic, our brain offers up a list of related experiences, jokes, stories, or insights. That's fine when you're shooting the breeze with your buddies. But in a customer alignment meeting, when your mission is to uncover the customer's goals and challenges, you need to focus on the words coming out of the customer's mouth, not on your internal fun-time story generator. No, those internal thoughts need to be let go of, so you can focus on the customer.

If this is difficult for you, I suggest cultivating what's called mindfulness. Try the mindfulness guidance outlined in the book *Start Where You Are* by Pema Chodron. Her meditation techniques give a power boost to active listening. Practice the techniques at home, when you are alone. Then bring it into the conference room once you're comfortable using it.

Here's what you do. Set a timer for five minutes. Sit down with good posture. Lengthen your spine, strengthen your belly, and pull your shoulders back and down. Now, focus on your breath, counting each one. Say to yourself, "Breathe in, breathe out one. Breathe in, breathe out two. . . ."

Eventually, your mind will wander. Perhaps you catch yourself thinking about your car. You think something like *Oh, it may be time to change the oil.* Oops! You caught yourself thinking about your car and not thinking about your breathing. Your mind wandered. What now?

First, be gentle with yourself. This is what our brains do. They generate thoughts and feed them to our consciousness. You probably *should* change the oil in your car, even if now is not the time to think about it.

So instead of darting off to the garage, remain seated and imagine writing your thought on a scrap of paper. Write something simple, like "oil change." Now, imagine attaching the note to a string hanging from a balloon and releasing the balloon into the wind. Let the breeze carry your thought off into the sky. Let it go. Let it be gone.

Now, come back to your breath. "Breathe in, breathe out one. . . . "

Repeat this until the alarm buzzes. Every time your thoughts wander, mentally write them down and then release them on a balloon. The key is to practice the act of letting go. By visualizing something as real as a balloon and note flying off with the cleansing wind, you trick your brain into truly letting the thought go. Keep doing this regularly and consider extending your meditation time to ten minutes or more. This mind training might help you focus and gain clarity in more areas of your life than simply aligning with customers. Once you've gotten the hang of it, use this technique in meetings to gently put your attention back on the customer.

Get comfortable with discomfort.

You may have a strong feeling about a customer. Perhaps he's been a real jerk to you in the past. He's pushy, calling every day to obtain product before anyone else, using every tactic in the book to squeeze every last dime out of his pricing. You feel like it's a one-sided relationship and you're always on the side that's getting the short end of the stick. You're resentful.

Hey, these are valid feelings. I sympathize. However, when you're uncovering the customer's goals and challenges, it's imperative you put aside these feelings. As we had discussed in chapter five about setting the right mind-set, try imagining that you are Sherlock Holmes to overcome this. It's silly but, incredibly, it works. I imagine that I, like Mr. Holmes, am wholly dispassionate. My intentions are singular: to collect indisputable facts that I can use to solve the great mystery before me: What are the customer's goals and challenges? Go all out: Imagine you wear a tweed deerstalker, are puffing on a briar pipe packed to the brim with aromatic tobacco. Imagine yourself, Mr. Holmes, sitting at the conference room table with your customer. It's not so bad anymore, is it? Now get to work. Ask your questions and collect your clues. Even when you're not feeling so comfortable with the situation.

Cultivate curiosity.

This is about getting outside of your own storyline and getting interested in your customer's. Look at her. Where's she from? What does she care about? With your detective's hat still on, imagine you're holding up a magnifying glass to your customer. For the next few hours your mission is to step out of your world and get into hers. Do whatever it takes to cultivate curiosity to learn about her and especially her goals and challenges at work and within her marketplace.

If your customer expresses views that contrast with your own, you may find that your detective's hat fails to detach you from your own point of view. In such a case, imagine you are in a theater troupe and your task is to play the role of your customer. You must see the world from her perspective in order to effectively portray her in the play. Don't worry. After the meeting, you'll duly snap back to your own point of view. There's no harm in abandoning it for the sake of learning.

You may find some of the tips contained in the *Psychology Today* article "Cultivating Curiosity" by Elizabeth Svoboda (September 1, 2006) helpful in reframing boring meetings and forgetting your fears.

Corporate meetings needn't be boring. Seek out details you might otherwise miss. For example, while people are filing into the meeting room, guess where each person bought his or her shirt. Or, during the meeting, observe how each person takes notes—on a laptop, tablet, or paper. Try to guess where people grew up. Come up with your own creative curiosity to follow. If it's corporately correct, you can even bring it up as a topic at a break.

Look out for nonverbal cues.

When you're busy taking notes and intently listening to the conversation, you may feel you have little bandwidth to spare for observing tone of voice or body language. In fact, your brain can't help but take stock of nonverbal cues. A study in 1967, "Decoding of Inconsistent Communications" by Dr. Alert Mehrabian, demonstrated that as much as 55 percent of communication can be attributed to body language and 35 percent to tone. Many other findings have backed up these numbers. This means it pays to pay attention to nonverbal cues you're sending and also to nonverbal feedback you're receiving from the customer. The more you make note of body language and tone, the more you may find your communication improves. Here are some tips:

If the customer's legs and arms are crossed or she is turned to the side and looking away as you talk, she is in a defensive posture and may not be fully engaged or forthcoming. You might want to back off the current line of questioning and return to a subject that's more comfortable.

Or be direct. State your observation and ask what's going on: "You seem uncomfortable. What are your concerns on this topic?" When you're having trouble reading a situation, try restating your understanding thus far. Say what you've heard and directly ask the customer whether you've comprehended the full message. This works wonders at getting you back on the same page.

Body language goes both ways. When you address the customer, sit with your body square to the table, open your arms to a comfortable width, and minimize fidgeting. Hold your shoulders back and down. This does a few things. For one, it opens up your heart and mind to incoming information. For another, it communicates presence and focus. Look the customer in the eye during the conversation, for a few seconds at a time, periodically. This improves the connection and demonstrates interest. Just remember to blink and look away occasionally. You don't want to make it weird.

Identify the feeling.

It's not just body language that communicates upset conditions, of course. Sometimes customers or clients come right out and say they're angry, frustrated, or disappointed. Any of these can put your team on the defensive. The trick is to focus on uncovering what's behind the feeling so that you don't get lost making excuses or otherwise defending yourself. Protecting your ego is not the agenda here. Your objective is to ask questions that give the customer time and space to fully express the needs behind the emotions.

Before we get into what to do, now's a good time to point out that preparation is the key to avoiding such scenarios altogether. In Chapter Two: "Roles and Responsibilities," you saw how to avoid setting up customer alignment meetings with customers until sticky current issues have been resolved. By the time you meet, there should be no outstanding ill will. If you come across an angry customer, it means the organizers failed to identify an issue or it means a problem cropped up between scheduling and holding the meeting. Whatever the reason, encountering such an upset customer should be infrequent. That said, it happens. Here's how to proceed should it happen to you.

Marshall B. Rosenberg's book *Nonviolent Communication* is a useful guide for working with upset customers. Rosenberg prescribes a four-step process for communication.

1. Observe without evaluating. It may seem counterintuitive, but the first step is to identify that the customer is upset and say so. You might say, "You seem upset." This statement can be like shaking a soda can and opening it: explosive. Put on your goggles and prepare to be sprayed. A tirade is coming, and that's good. The worst thing you could do is ignore the anger and have the customer go through a whole meeting with bottled-up emotions. A customer like this will be closed off and unwilling to share. Therefore, your job is to provide a forum where the customer can work through each and every feeling. Your job is to listen and understand what the underlying needs are. Don't worry; you don't need to fix anything. You need to listen and understand. The first step is to simply uncover their story and state your observations.

2. Identify feelings. Let's say that the customer replied to your observation by saying, "Damn right, I'm upset. I was told I was buying a fully tested and verified product. But just minutes into use, it was painfully clear that was not the case!"

Here, you may feel the urge to defend your company or start to solve the problem. It's too early for that. First, you must identify the feelings and let the customer express them. Try to guess at what the customer is feeling and ask if that's correct. You might say, "So you felt hurt and angry."

The customer may say, "Yeah, you guys really let me down. Your representative assured me this product would be rock-solid. It makes all your products suspect!"

You say, "You've lost confidence in us."

Customer, "You bet I have! It's like you pulled the rug out from under us. It's distressing and taxing our schedule and energy. Now we have to go back and verify every component from your company to make sure they'll perform as expected. It's going to be a lot of work."

3. Identify needs underlying feelings. The customer is angry, disappointed, and even distressed. Now it's time to uncover their unfulfilled needs.

In this example, you might say, "You'd counted on us, and by failing to communicate that we were shipping you a beta product, we led you to believe that it would work out of the box. When it didn't, your need for the quality of your product was compromised. Is that about right?"

"Well, yeah, for us to deliver high-quality product to our customers, on schedule, we have to be able to rely on the quality of your products."

You just heard another underlying need. See if you got it right by asking, "When our products failed to meet your expectations, it caused you to slip your schedule?"

"Of course. And in our business, time to market is everything. If we slip by even a week, our entire project could be cut. We're already late to market, and management is breathing down our necks. It's do or die. We can't afford a schedule slip!"

4. Identify concrete actions in order to fulfill the underlying need. At this point, you know the customer is upset, confidence has been lost, and their schedule has been affected. Furthermore, you've learned that the stakes are high. You may be tempted to jump into action and try to fix everything. Or you may be tempted to admonish the company representative who misled the poor customer. Instead, it's time to learn what they would like you to do.

You can say, "At this point, you're distressed, have lost confidence in us and, worst of all, your schedule has been delayed. What specific actions could we take to make this right?"

You've invited the customer to state what they expect. Note that you are not signing up to do everything they ask for. Think of this as the discovery phase of a negotiation. You're simply identifying various possible actions they would interpret as making up for whatever caused the initial discord.

The customer might answer, "Well, we're close to finishing the verification. Your support team is helping us. I know they're busy, but I really need them to prioritize our project. If you could make it clear to your management that the work they're doing is critical for us and make sure they have the time and resources to finish the verification work, that'd go a long way."

That was reasonable. But now's not the time to sign up for the action. Now is the time for active listening, specifically, an active listening after question: "Anything else?"

The customer answers, "Yeah, in the future, I suggest your sales reps learn more about how we use your products before they assure us that everything's fine. As far as I can tell, they assumed we were using the default mode, which, having worked with the support team, I can tell you, works out of the box just fine. But we twiddle the settings in user mode. That configuration hadn't been fully tested before you shipped us product. Your sales team was too eager to make the sale. They were hasty, and we paid the price."

Now's the time to ask another ALAQ. But this time precede it by restating what you've heard. "So you'd like us to prioritize the verification work with our support team, ensure their managers understand the importance of the work they're doing, and talk with the sales representatives to make sure they gather more information about your usage case before assuring you everything will work. Anything else?"

"No. To be honest, if you did those things, we'd be square."

At this point, you've provided a forum where the customer had all the space and opportunity to air their emotions, needs, and requests for reparations. You may notice that the tension in the room has lifted and the customer is more relaxed. You heard the root problem.

If you think that the requests are reasonable and doable, you can tell the customer that you'll follow up with the sales team and with the support team's management. If, however, you would rather not sign up for those action items, then tell the customer that you'll want to carve out a few minutes at the end of the meeting to review these as well as other actions from the day. Perhaps at a break, you can privately communicate with the sales team and support team management. This is one of the perks of holding a customer alignment meeting at your headquarters. Oftentimes, the best people to address a customer's needs are right there. Of course, you'll want to be diplomatic. Work with the sales team and support team's management to come up with a solution they're comfortable with. Whatever you do, don't sign anyone up for an action item unless they agree to it first. And, remember, as you interact with the upset customer, make sure you write down what you hear. It's at this emotionally charged moment that they need to know they're being heard and understood. Taking notes goes a long way toward assuring them that you're not only listening, but you're also taking their words seriously.

Be the duck.

My friend, a website developer, grew annoyed with my barrage of questions about a site she'd set up for a charity I was starting. One day, I asked her a question, only to answer it myself midway through describing the problem. She said, "Get a duck," then sent me a link to an article, *LiveJournal*'s "Ask the Duck" (January 6, 2012).

In this piece, the author recalled the early days of his career when he kept pestering his boss with questions about sprinkler systems they were designing. Eventually, his boss told him to direct his questions to a toy duck on a shelf in the office. Feeling stupid, he nevertheless asked the duck his question out loud. Midsentence, the solution dawned on him.

There's something about hearing yourself work through a problem out loud. It's as if your mind processes it with fresh perspective. Newfound creativity swooshes in as you expand the framework for solving a problem. In a customer alignment meeting, the right question can prompt the customer to talk through their situation from a fresh perspective. The simple act of giving voice to their ideas puts the situation in a new light. It can be a miraculous conversation. Verbally walking through the problem can lead the customer to see the situation from a totally new perspective.

Often when customers come to CA meetings, they find themselves explaining their situation out loud, from a ten-thousand-foot view, for the first time. They grow excited as they talk through their situation from this new perspective. At this point, the uncovering team is the duck. What does a stuffed duck do? That's right: it keeps its mouth shut and lets the customer talk and talk through this land of self-discovery. The duck listens. The duck sits still. In your case, of course, you're a special kind of duck who simultaneously writes down everything it hears. Occasionally, you, the duck, might quack briefly with a follow-up question such as "What else?" or "Anything else?"

Ask active listening questions, get the customer taking, and then shut up and listen. Be the duck.

CHAPTER TEN

Aligning Skills: Making a Record

"If it's not written down, it didn't happen."
—*Journal of Community Nursing*

AT THIS POINT in the book, I request permission to treat you as a hostile witness. No, I don't think you're emotionally combative. As far as I can tell, you're a perfectly lovely person. However, I'd guess that you're similar to the majority of the people I've worked with. I'm going to assume you don't take regular and rigorous notes. That will have to be rectified for customer alignment meetings. To gain the most from customer interactions, you need to record all customer comments and create accurate meeting notes for immediate distribution to all who participated as soon as the meeting ends.

For this chapter, I'm putting you on cross-examination. That means I'm allowed to pose leading questions and steer you to specific conclusions that I want to convince you of. You can decide, at the end of this chapter, whether I've made my case.

WHO, ME?

My colleague, a senior manager, sat across the lunch table. He bubbled with enthusiasm. "That customer meeting was awesome! Man, there's nothing like hearing straight from the customer!"

"That good, huh?" I steadied myself and asked, "Where can I find the notes?" I braced for one of three typical answers.

"Well," he said, "I assume someone else took notes. Anyway, I don't need notes. It's all in here." He tapped his temple. Sensing my disillusionment, he half-heartedly backtracked. "Maybe I'll type them up later."

Wow, he nailed it. He gave all three of the most common and delusional excuses from people who don't file notes. Let's take a look at each one.

Delusion #1: Assuming Others Are Taking Notes

The truth is they aren't. To believe your colleagues are taking diligent notes is to believe in magical note-taking minions. They don't exist.

It's no longer the era of *Mad Men*, when creative executives had their secretaries take notes on their behalf in every meeting. I've worked in the semiconductor industry since 1996, and in all that time I've not once seen someone's administrative assistant taking notes for them. Ever.

Perhaps some people regard note-taking to be beneath them. Still others succumb to bystander apathy, a phenomenon in which individuals fail to act when other people are present. As the head count of bystanders increases, the probability of individual action decreases. Similarly, in a customer alignment meeting, if note-taking responsibilities are at all ambiguous and head count is large, there's a good chance that no one will take notes.

Delusion #2: Believing One Has a Photographic Memory

People who say "It's all in my head" believe their brains are reliable and searchable storage devices. I'm here to tell you they aren't.

Fidelity refers to the accuracy of a copy. A few decades ago, hi-fi audio recordings were all the rage. In the modern day, audio sample rates and precisions exceed a human's capacity to detect significant differences between an original and its copy. Everything is hi-fi in the modern world. Unless you're talking about our brains.

Unlike a digital audio recording, the accuracy of my colleague's memory is supermega low fidelity. The truth is human recall is inaccurate and misshapen by confirmation bias.

Given the way our brains encode, consolidate, and recall information, none of us should fully trust our memories. The process of memory storage is fascinating and horrifying.

"Okay, so what? Memory fades over time. It's not a big deal," you say, adding, "I remember the salient bits." Ah yes, but the scary thing is we don't simply forget stuff or lose a few details. Data erosion is one of many phenomena that renders our memory unreliable. Here are the others: we store false fabricated memories, biased memories, and memory fragments. Our brains, unbeknownst to us, take liberty to "smooth the narrative" or "fill in the blanks" while recalling episodic memories ("Retelling Is Not the Same As Recalling: Implications for Memory" by Elizabeth J. Marsh). Our brains invoke schemas that tease out storylines resonant with preexisting notions, all while letting go pesky irreconcilable details. This filtered memory is the one that gets stored for later.

This goes on without our realizing it.

And there's more! Your brain is highly suggestible and can be made to fabricate memories. It takes only a few subtle comments from an outsider to cause you to store a false memory. In fact, in diabolical experiments, researchers such as Elizabeth Loftus were able to install false memories in 30 percent to 50 percent of their subjects. Scary stuff.

Usually, you don't make up memories out of whole cloth. Instead, your brain mutates memories. The brain is presented with a staggering number of opportunities to meddle. From encoding to storing, consolidation to recall, the frontal lobes and hippocampus work together to prune and distort information at every transmission. By the time you recall a story, weeks after the event, the only thing you can be sure of is your retelling is super-duper lo-fi.

More than a few people I've worked with have claimed photographic memories. They typically point to their foreheads and say, "It's all in here." This is a delusion. In truth, our brains are unreliable storage devices.

Delusion #3: I'll Type Up My Notes Later

The action item of writing up meeting notes drops down to-do lists everywhere like car keys into a storm drain. Once they've dropped below a certain point, they're gone forever.

I suspect that people fail to type up notes because, while important, the task rarely feels urgent. As time passes, urgent tasks crowd out the note task. People who succumb to delusion #3 prioritize these "urgent" issues and never get to the important long-term improvement stuff, such as typing up notes. The problem is if there's no record of a meeting, it may as well not have happened. Failing to take notes wastes everyone's time and can lead to wrong conclusions. "If it's not written, it didn't happen."

Missed Opportunities

When notes are not recorded or stored in a centralized and searchable location, the company loses out. Perhaps our colleague heard some trivial-seeming bits of information. He'll quickly forget them, but in some corner of the corporation those bits of information may be highly valued. If not written down, they can't benefit anyone.

Also, if the data is stored in a person's brain, there's only one way for it to be shared: through that person's time and effort. Imagine yourself in this position. Do you really want to be the on-demand server for distributing customer comments to the wider organization? And who would know what information they could retrieve from you if you didn't advertise the meeting contents? You may be able to act on a subset of the information, but you can't possibly know how valuable every bit is to every person in all departments. When you keep all the customer's comments in your head, you limit the usefulness of what was learned.

In addition, delaying taking notes reduces their completeness. Information that would be captured if you took notes in the moment may degrade when you wait to record your impressions. We've learned about some ways our brains distort memories. But sometimes the memory never has a chance to be made. During a meeting, a door might open or the fan might churn on. The customer might state something in a high-pitched tone that is difficult to hear. Three minutes later, you realize you haven't heard a word as you awake from daydreaming about a hilarious cat video your niece sent you that morning. You tune back in. Two minutes later, you're dismayed to find you're distracted again.

Distractions cause whole chunks of conversation to be missed. The thoughts don't even have a chance to get stored in memory because they are never heard.

Encoding errors often result from misinterpretation. It's astounding how often we hear what we want to hear rather than what is said. Our brains are pattern-recognition machines, and they love to jump to conclusions before all the information is in. Do you ever find yourself filling in other people's sentences when they pause? These fill-in-the blank predictions are based upon preexisting schemas stored in your head. You call them up constantly because your brain relies on them to make sense of the world. For the most part, they're helpful. But they can disrupt the storing of accurate memories. These schemas prompt us to cherry-pick parts of the story line that resonate with what is already in our heads. They filter out new, subtly differing information. And yet if you're trying to uncover customer goals and challenges, it's the discordant and unexpected information that is exactly what you want to capture. Our reliance on schemas can make us miss the information we're after.

If you take notes and periodically check your understanding by summarizing what you heard out loud, you may be astonished to find the customer arguing with you. They might say, "No, you missed the most important point!" And that's great!

Storing Memories Is Error Prone

When you observe something and store the memory, it's not a one-time event. Memory storage is multistaged, and each stage can introduce errors. A single memory can be batted between brain regions hundreds of times. With each transfer, it's vulnerable to pruning and distortions, while simultaneously those distortions are reinforced.

First, a memory is put into short-term memory. This is typically an auditory and relatively hi-fi copy. If the memory is subsequently recalled, schemas act as a filter, selecting which bits of the memory to pull and which bits to discard.

At night, the brain consolidates memory, whereby episodic memory fragments bounce from frontal lobe to hippocampus repeatedly, and, in doing so further bias the memory to match existing schemas. By the time you wake up, some portion of a very lo-fi memory might be stored in long-term memory. I say *might* because it is a gamble which memories will be deemed worth storing by the hippocampus and frontal lobes.

"Retelling Is Not the Same As Reading: Implications for Memory" by Elizabeth J. Marsh of Duke University explains how another common practice alters recollection: retelling. Long story short, when retelling an experience, people tend to report the items that they think their audience will find most interesting. Fair enough. The scary thing is this retelling introduces yet another memory-pattern filter. Later, people tend to remember the story they retold rather than the initial story they experienced. In other words, when retelling a story, we create a schema that we imagine exists within our audience's collective brain and adapt our memory to it. That's crazy! But it's human.

Remember our financial planner named Bob in chapter six? Say one of Bob's clients came in for her quarterly meeting and discussed many topics: she'd taken on a new heir, she felt skittish about the market and thought it might be good to raise cash, she'd been seeing a new golf pro and had shaved three strokes off of her handicap. Bob didn't take notes.

Now, imagine that after the meeting, Bob runs into a coworker, a scratch golfer. Bob recounts details about his customer's new golf pro. The coworker is incredulous that Bob's client could improve her handicap so quickly. They agree to hit the links that weekend. Bob proceeds to his desk, becomes distracted by urgent e-mails, and doesn't get around to typing up his meeting notes for another three days.

How likely is it that Bob will write up the customer comments regarding her new heir? Or her change in risk comfort? Given that he's recounted a version of the story that omits these comments, there's a good chance he'll forget some of the salient points of her message.

Solving the Problem

The antidote is to create a culture of verbatim note-taking. It sounds easy, but if there's a culture of winging it, getting people to put pen to paper will likely be a monumental task. Taking notes is an optimal way to retain "high-fidelity" records of what customers actually say.

If you don't make note-taking part of the process, you may as well not hold customer alignment meetings. In fact, if you have no intention of taking verbatim notes, you may be better off not talking with the customer at all. Without notes, you risk people recalling distorted memories that could point your company in the wrong direction.

A culture of note-taking can fix this. Then, the next time you ask an excited colleague where the notes are, you may be pointed to the record. There, you'll be able to read what actually happened in the meeting.

So roll up your sleeves, because I'm going to tell you exactly how to take high-fidelity notes.

HOW TO TAKE NOTES

Notes form the raw data output from customer alignment meetings. They should be accurate, be unbiased, and reflect exactly what the customer said. In fact, a copy will be sent to the customer soon after the meeting. In order to create high-fidelity notes, it's critical that everyone on the aligning team learn how to take notes in a consistent way and that scribe roles be clearly understood and assigned.

Verbatim Notes

If you're tasked with taking notes (aka a "scribe"), you're expected to record the customer's verbatim comments as well as action items during the session in which you've been assigned responsibility. During your session, write down as much of what the customer says as you can. Take notes in the customer's voice, replicating exact phrases, jargon, and lingo.

Don't interpret. Don't record what you think the customer meant. Record what was actually said, even if you believe the customer was in error. You can always ask to make sure the customer meant what was said. When you record the subsequent answer, the correction will be reflected in your notes.

There are two reasons why notes must be in the customer's own voice: to create a high-fidelity record of what was heard and to assist in active listening question restatements.

Notes are source data. They're unfiltered, raw evidence. As a detective, your job is to collect unsullied clues. The team can interpret meanings later. In this verbatim word-for-word form, the notes are as reliable as they're going to get.

Furthermore, notes should be free of commentary. If you feel you must note a parenthetical observation, clearly mark it as such.

Tactically, ALAQs (active listening after questions)—remember those?—get a power boost when you restate your understanding of what the customer said while using bits of the customer's verbatim phrasing. They can't argue with their own words—for long, at least. You may be surprised how often they try to. And when they correct you, write down what they say. Oftentimes these corrections get you to the real story.

Verbatim notes convey more than interpreted notes ever could. For example, what if a customer was exasperated that a particular device vendor had them "by the ovaries"? Could a neutralized translation express this any better? The customer's original expression often tells the story better than you ever could. So use it.

When the customer hears you restate their exact words, you demonstrate that you are recording their comments with fidelity. They're being heard and have every reason to share more.

Recruit Many Notetakers

In effective customer alignment meetings, note-taking duties revolve from person to person throughout the day between rotating attendees. Here's why: Assigning a single person as a scribe for more than an hour or two will result in incomplete notes. For one thing, the notes will wither as the day progresses; it's fatiguing taking notes all day. Besides, if you assign a single person as notetaker for an entire day, you may give them the perception that they've been cast into the position of meeting lackey.

Rather, make note-taking a team activity. Spread the responsibility around. Each stakeholder should shoulder at least some of this daunting duty. I suggest assigning a mix of session and topic scribes.

Session Scribes

Imagine the customer will be with you for eight hours. You've scheduled four one-hundred-minute sections with breaks in between. I recommend assigning one scribe per session who is responsible for recording everything the customer says as well as all action items during their designated one-hundred-minute period. This is a reasonable thing to ask of team members. Taking notes for four hundred minutes is not.

Subject Matter Expert Scribes

A topic-specific or subject matter expert scribe takes notes that touch on his core areas of expertise. That applies to every attendee no matter their level or specialty. For example, you might have one person take notes that have to do with quality and reliability. Another person may take notes on core product functions. It will all depend on the direction of an attendee's knowledge and expertise. These scribes do not necessarily record other topics, and they do not limit their note-taking to a particular time frame. Rather, they focus exclusively on their particular bailiwick.

On one hand, SME scribes can be the best notetakers because they know the topic. On the other hand, they can be the worst for the same reason. They might omit comments they regard as common knowledge, even when they're the only ones who have that knowledge. Their familiarity also may have their notes jumping to conclusions because their brains anticipate patterns to be matched with preexisting schemas.

Once during the break in a customer alignment meeting, I asked to see an SME's notes. He said he hadn't taken any because he already knew what the client was going to say. Facepalm!

That's why SME scribes should be supplemental to session scribes. With two sets of notes, the truth has a better chance of emerging during the post-CA meeting. An SME's perspective can be a valuable supplement to the meeting record. And don't forget, if you are attending a CA meeting in your capacity as an expert, it is incumbent upon you to take notes on your area of specialization, even if no one has assigned you note-taking duties.

Who should be a scribe?

Consider asking each topic presenter to bring along a trusted lieutenant to record notes. It could be a mentoring opportunity.

The only requirement is that this person have taken the training included in this book. In addition, a subject matter expert scribe should be somewhat familiar with the topic to be discussed. If head count is an issue, however, you may want people who are already attending to handle the note-taking.

But if head count isn't an issue, a junior employee can gain useful perspective in a customer alignment meeting. Sitting in as a scribe—session or SME—is a chance to hear directly from highly influential and knowledgeable customers. It's also a chance to witness CA skills being put to practice. In time, SME scribes could become regular SME presenters. Bringing in scribes as part of a mentoring program has the additional benefit of instilling confidence in the team. They'll know that a competent alternate could take on the role of expert presenter in the meeting if an emergency arises.

No matter whom you recruit, confirm that each scribe understands exactly what's expected of them: how to take notes; what specific notes to record; how to clean up notes; and where to send the notes after the meeting. A guide to each of these steps follows.

Mechanics of Note-taking

Whether you use a tablet, laptop, or paper and pen, here are a few tips that may help.

- Make heavy use of abbreviations for efficiency. For example, instead of writing *market*, write *mkt*.

- Use acronyms from your business as long as they are well known. Examples: B2B (business to business), ROI (return on investment), API (application programming interface). Doing so will improve your speed.

- Borrow acronyms from social media. Here's a list I use regularly:

    - IIRC = if I recall correctly
    - AFAIK = as far as I know
    - IMO = in my opinion
    - BAE = before anyone else
    - IDC = I don't care
    - IDK = I don't know
    - NBD = no big deal
    - PPL = people
    - TIL = today I learned
    - SMH = shaking my head
    - TL; DR = too long; didn't read (short summary follows this acronym)

- Make up your own acronyms. Just be sure you'll be able to decipher them later when you clean up your notes. TVHMBTO may have seemed clever at the time, but that isn't a guarantee it will mean anything to you later.

- Omit articles, prepositions, and conjunctions that can otherwise be inferred.

- If you use pen and paper, learn shorthand substitutions. Here are shorthand marks from the Pitman shorthand method. Some of these translate to typing; others not so much.

\ = to	**o** = is/his	**.** = the		= it/it's
\ = of	**o** = as/	**·** = an	/ = and

Imagine the customer says, "The market is moving fast. My opinion is that in the next two years, we will need to be able to double our core frequency and operate at four hundred megahertz or more. Plus, we need at least 20 percent margin and, if I recall correctly from the next-generation chassis specifications, our power budget will remain the same as it is today."

You needn't write down every word. The following is much more concise, while still verbatim:

". mkt mv fast. IMO, in 2 yr, need 2x perf, fmax >400MHz + >20% mrgn. IIRC next gen chassis specs = pwr budget = same as today."

If you were able to make sense of my shorthand, then you'll likely be able to transpose these notes back to the original words with acceptable accuracy later.

Don't worry about recording comments from colleagues.

When you're taking notes, I don't care that Jamie from the finance department expresses prognostications about the death of mortgage-backed securities. Jamie works for the company and can express that opinion to relevant people inside the company anytime. The whole point of this meeting is to hear the customer. Write down what the customer says, and unless Jamie's comments contribute to the context of the customer comments, leave them out. If you feel your teammate's comments provide useful information, then clearly note them parenthetically along with Jamie's name.

Use your best judgment on whether to record the question asked.

The question is usually implied by the customer's answer. Use your best judgment here. If customer comments stand up alone, don't worry about recording the question. However, if the comments make no sense without the question, then by all means note the question that was asked.

That said, writing down verbatim questions could potentially be used to improve the team's questioning skills overall, as improvements on phrasing could be discussed in internal review meetings.

Take notes from the customer's perspective.

You are taking verbatim notes, so they should automatically be in the customer's voice. As you're writing, strive to do so as if you are the customer. Try to see the world from his worldview. By doing so, you may come up with questions that emanate from a genuine place of curiosity as you try to fill in the full picture. This is Jedi mind-trick stuff. Give it a try.

What technology to use?

My preference is to use a tablet with an application called Sound-Note. It's quiet and saves me time tidying my notes later. Added bonus: I get to avoid reading my awful handwriting. One cool part is that SoundNote makes an audio recording and synchronizes it with the typed notes. This is enormously useful after the meeting, when cleaning up the notes.

Note: if you use an app or device that makes an audio recording of the meeting, be sure to obtain permission beforehand. Let the customer know that your word processing application records audio and ask if that's okay. Explain that the purpose of the audio recording is simply to make sure your notes are accurate. You also might say that the recording will remain in your hands and will not be shared with anyone.

While a tablet is my preference, I understand that not everyone likes tapping away on a screen. Also, if you're a wiz at shorthand, a tablet may not be necessary or lend itself to your note-taking techniques.

It's always fine to take notes in a paper notebook, as long as you're willing to type them up right after the meeting. The main advantage of paper and pen is the silence. Even when you're using a tablet, the tapping of fingers on the screen makes some amount of noise. Paper wins in this area. Also, paper and pen are ideal for drawing diagrams. I've seen some people use drawing software for this. I invite you to try whatever technology is out today.

A laptop is okay, but be careful. If too many people are tapping away on laptops, the noise can impede communication. An open laptop also introduces a physical barrier between you and the customer. Furthermore, it can goad you into looking at your screen and not at the customer. Incoming e-mails and other pop-up alerts can further distract you. In this middle focus, you may be tempted to get some work done even as the conversation carries on. Each of these factors degrades personal connection.

Note-taking technologies are evolving quickly, so I'm not going to go into details on the pros and cons of every existing app. Try different options. Observe how each affects the conversation, connection, and noise level. If a new technology doesn't get in the way and assists you in taking accurate and verbatim notes, go for it.

Immediately type up notes and send them in.

If you're assigned the task of taking notes, take the time to type them up into a legible form as soon as physically possible. That ideally means directly afterward. Don't be like one of my colleagues who agreed to take notes during a meeting. The next morning, I e-mailed, asking for the notes. Five minutes later he was at my desk, holding out his engineering notepad. He opened it to a page full of illegible chicken scratch. He magnanimously offered, "You can scan these into the system. Just have the notebook back to me by the end of the day."

I pushed the notebook back at him. "No, my friend. You can type the notes up yourself. Post them to the customer repository, as explained in the meeting invitation."

I never saw his notes.

Don't be like that colleague.

My friend Robert Kirby of Kirby Leadership Training once told me he schedules tasks he doesn't want to do at the start of his morning. He likens these tasks to eating a frog. Before doing the fun stuff, he eats the frog. If you are ever an official scribe, you, too, should eat the frog.

During the CA meeting, you may have written sparse bullet points down to capture the comments that strike you as important. After the meeting, fill in the details that you failed to capture during it—right away! Whatever you do, don't sleep on it. Our brains scrub much of the day's short-term memory when we sleep. If you wait until later, even if just the next day, you risk losing important information. You can even take into account the time needed for writing up notes afterward when scheduling the CA meeting so that your visiting client doesn't eat up the time needed to memorialize their comments.

Clean up your notes.

You've typed up your notes from the meeting. You've relived the customer's goals and challenges as you edited the pages. That's great! You're done. Right? No. Take another few minutes to run a spell check and grammar check. Fix punctuation issues and errors. It doesn't have to be perfect, but it does need to be readable. Also, make sure that any parenthetical statements or observations are clearly marked as such and, if possible, note who made them. Keep in mind that the notes will be forwarded to the customer, so remove any personal commentary that the customer might not appreciate.

Don't make the host or meeting organizer edit your notes. They'll be juggling them from all the scribes, which could be ten people. The host is responsible for typing up the summary of the meeting. Don't make them fix your spelling and grammatical mistakes too.

Record all "internal eyes only" comments in a separate document and put them aside until you attend the post-CA meeting. By holding off on sharing them until after the notes have gone to the customer, you can be sure they won't inadvertently be included in the customer's copy.

Writing up and cleaning up notes is a frog task if there ever was one. I never met anyone who enjoyed writing them. Don't put it on your to-do list; just do it. Type them up as soon as you physically can, either during the CA meeting or immediately after it, to fill in missing bits or for handwritten notes.

Whatever you do, don't wait a week to type up and send in your notes, when your memories will be less fresh. Be a considerate teammate. Get your notes into the system within twenty-four hours. Just eat that frog already!

CHAPTER ELEVEN

Aligning Skills: Beyond the Basics

"Once you get trust and rapport, you get insight and answers." —Andy Turudic, Altera Corporation

So FAR we've covered the basics of questioning, listening to the customer's answers, and taking notes reflecting their views. Now we turn our attention to more advanced skills.

DEMONSTRATING CREDIBILITY

Customers invest in a conversation when they realize two things. First is when they realize you speak the same language. This means you understand industry-specific jargon, you're aware of historical events associated with the topics under discussion, or you and your team have similar experiences in overcoming challenges associated with a similar job. Second is when they come to realize they're talking with a team that can influence the company. Make sure your team is made up of these people and demonstrate their qualities straightaway. Do this at the outset of the meeting, during introductions. It can be as simple as having each attendee share what projects they're working on and what they hope to get out of the meeting.

There's a paradox at work here. In a customer alignment meeting, the first order of business is to focus on the customer *prior* to talking about you. So how do you demonstrate credibility without making the conversation about you?

Very carefully and very quickly.

In my experience, when people are asked to demonstrate credibility, they tend to take it too far. "Oh, you want me to talk about me? Can do . . ." and they're off. They list their experience and accomplishments and then elaborate on what interests them. Some people don't seem to know when to stop. They bogart the conversation, coming off as boorish, self-serving, or egotistical.

On the other hand, if you open the meeting with open-ended active listening questions, you may find the customer is unwilling to share. This is because they've no idea whom they're talking to. It's up to you to provide this information, but only just enough!

Keep it brief.

In William Shakespeare's *Hamlet*, Polonius says, "Brevity is the soul of wit." Ironically, he spoke these words amid an exceedingly loquacious monologue. Don't do as Polonius does; do what he says.

Later in the customer alignment meeting, well after uncovering the customer's situation, if you're a subject matter expert and your pet topic is on the list of topics to discuss, that's when you can dive into details about your work. However, at the outset of the meeting, state only as much information as is needed to communicate that you are worth talking to and no more.

If you have a story to tell and you think you can keep it brief, then consider sharing it. Get permission from the host beforehand. When in doubt, keep it brief—no more than one minute or two. Elaborate only when the host directs you to do so. Even then, your monologue should not exceed a couple of minutes. You've got an agenda to get to.

COMBATING CONFIRMATION BIAS

In chapter ten, I mentioned schemas. In this chapter we take a closer look. Schemas play a major role in confirmation bias. And confirmation bias must be overcome in a customer alignment setting.

A schema is a simplified representation of reality that we hold in our minds. We create and rely upon schemas in order to make sense of the world. Some schemas have names, like "chair." When you read that word, you instantly pull a schema and imagine a chair.

With schemas, we easily convey complex concepts without getting bogged down in details. There's so much information coming at us all the time, we couldn't possibly handle it all if we had to process each attribute of every object in view. Schemas play a key role in how we think.

But there's a dark side. What we gain in flexibility and lucidity, we lose in objectivity. Tackling confirmation bias is by far the most difficult of the aligning tricks to master, and much of the challenge is presented by schemas doing their job: providing mental shortcuts.

We are constantly pattern-matching our experience against schemas. As a result, we often hear what we *expect* to hear. A strong belief system might have us hearing what we *want* to hear. None of us are exempt. We're all guilty of cherry-picking facts that support our preconceived ideas. It's simply how our minds work.

Some of us, however, intentionally seek out information that supports our beliefs. We ask loaded questions to prompt answers we want to hear. The hallmarks of these fishing expeditions are closed-ended questions that steer customers toward specific answers which might be used to justify a pet project, for instance. People who ask such questions are contemptuous of the customer, the truth, and the team.

Remember Cunningham bombs? When deployed, these sacrifice your dignity in exchange for key information. The beauty of the Cunningham bomb is the information you gain is generally unbiased, truthful, and useful. Contrast that with casting out a line on a fishing expedition with a closed-ended question. In this case, you sacrifice your integrity for biased and often erroneous information.

Take the example of William J. Casey. He was Ronald Reagan's campaign manager and later CIA director. Before Reagan took office as president of the United States, Casey read *The Terror Network* by Claire Sterling. This book connected the dots between various news articles that, taken together, seemed to link the Soviet Union to global terrorist organizations. These revelations outraged Casey, and he shared the book with friends and colleagues.

Soon after his swearing-in ceremony, he called a meeting with Melvin A. Goodman, then CIA division chief and head of Soviet affairs. Casey asked Goodman to corroborate Sterling's facts and conclusions. Goodman said he couldn't do that. Casey demanded to know why not. Here's an excerpt from an interview with Adam Curtis in the BBC documentary *The Power of Nightmares*:

MELVIN GOODMAN: When we looked through the book [*The Terror Network*], we found very clear episodes where CIA "black propaganda"—clandestine information that was designed under a covert action plan to be planted in European newspapers—were picked up and put in this book. A lot of it was made up. It was made up out of whole cloth.

INTERVIEWER (off-camera): You told [William Casey] this?

GOODMAN: We told him that, point blank. And we even had the operations people to tell Bill Casey this. I thought maybe this might have an impact, but all of us were dismissed. Casey had made up his mind. He knew the Soviets were involved in terrorism, so there was nothing we could tell him to disabuse him. Lies became reality.

Voice-over: In the end, Casey found a university professor who described himself as a terror expert, and he produced a dossier that confirmed that the hidden terror network did, in fact, exist.

This instance of confirmation bias is alarming. This wasn't a simple case of subconsciously missing a few facts. Casey's staff outright told him that they themselves had fabricated the evidence he relied on for his theory. Casey had to do convoluted and disingenuous mental gymnastics to justify what he did next. He purposefully disregarded the evidence before him and sought out alternate "facts" to support his steadfast view that Moscow was directing global terror. He went on to influence top leadership with his biased theories.

Of course, the stakes involved in aligning with customers are hardly as high as those of international diplomacy and foreign policy. Over time, however, if a corporation pursues justifying beliefs over discovering truth, chances increase that the wrong product will be built, market share ceded, and profits forgone.

When leaders and planners, instead, are rational stewards of their roles, they gather all relevant facts and evaluate them dispassionately.

Two people I worked with come to mind as stellar examples of this type: John Costello and Richard Cliff. They were vice presidents of engineering at Altera Corporation and attended my customer meetings regularly. They listened to customers with full interest.

Their questions suggested they sought information that bucked their personal views. John might ask a question like "You stated that you need x feature to achieve y. However, my understanding is that x is usually used to achieve z. Could you please elaborate on how using x to achieve y will get you closer to your goals?" Open-ended, not loaded, genuinely curious. Awesome.

I remember sitting next to Richard in one meeting when he poked me in the bicep. He leaned in and whispered that one of my colleagues had just asked a loaded leading question and that maybe I should correct our colleague's behavior. He said that he couldn't trust information collected in that manner. Double awesome.

Both of these gentlemen had profound respect for the customers. I never saw them try to put words in the customers' mouths. They had a job to do, and that was to build the right products for a given market at the right cost structure. Beyond that, they never seemed to have an agenda. It was evident that at some point in their lives each of them had learned how to minimize confirmation bias. Whether they worked at it or it came naturally, they were examples to follow.

And you can too!

Kellogg School of Management marketing professor Mohanbir Sawhney said, "To gain customer insights, we must understand that we are prisoners of what we know and what we believe." The bars of this prison are our schemas. But there's a way to unlock the gate and join the ranks of John and Richard.

Awareness of confirmation bias is a start, but it's insufficient. Stamping out confirmation bias takes conscious effort, vigilance, well-established processes, and disciplined habits. The following practices counteract confirmation bias. Some you already know, like taking verbatim notes, asking active listening questions, writing down questions prior to asking them, and sharing the raw notes with the customers after the customer alignment meeting. Here are some more tactics to help you avoid confirmation bias.

Be comfortable not knowing the answer.

Practice saying, "I don't know." Our inclination is to resolve the unknown and do it quickly. We trade truth for expedience in resolving uncertainty. We want to save a situation with an answer. It's okay to not know what the answer is. Double down with un-covering the customer's goals and challenges. Don't worry about tying up loose ends.

Create a culture of truth seekers.

If you're a leader of the group, go out of your way to appreciate the comments made by devil's advocates in the follow-up meeting. Demonstrate comfort and calm while holding two incompatible views at once. For example, acknowledge that many customers only care about cost while many other customers care about perfor-mance. These cases can coexist.

Actively seek out disconfirming data.

If a customer makes a statement that is contrary to conventional wisdom, ask follow-up questions to explore the comment further. This is easy to do when a customer says something that is obviously contrary. Those comments can be so jarring that missing them is impossible. Less obvious are comments that are only slightly off. Be on the lookout for those, and when the time is right ask for more details.

If you're a leader in the organization, go out of your way during follow-up meetings to compliment people who asked the customer about comments that were contrary to the conventional wisdom within your organization.

Keep in mind that often customer comments seem to be in line with your preconceived biases when, in fact, upon examination, they differ slightly. These are the comments that often go unexamined. As much as you tell yourself to keep an eye out for disconfirming comments, it is the slightly different information that will slip through. The only way to catch these is by taking verbatim notes and, as insurance, having both subject matter expert and session scribes recording the meeting at the same time.

Meet with customers who prefer your competition.

Talk to customers who hate you or clients with whom you have strained relationships. Strive to understand what they're trying to achieve, what their goals are, and in what ways they expect your competitors will help them make progress. Get them on a roll expressing their woes! Again, double down on uncovering more details surrounding comments that run counter to your beliefs. Ask for goals and challenges with an open heart and mind. Whatever you do, do not disparage the competition. That'll only make you look petty.

Adopt the mind-set of a scientist and don't get married to your plans.

The act of planning your business's strategic direction should be based on inductive reasoning, where you start with a set of future-focused objective observations and facts and then come to a conclusion based on those. That conclusion is assumed good until observations or facts come along that disprove it. This is in contrast to deductive reasoning, whereby a set of facts leads to a conclusion that is, itself, a provable fact. There's no way, alas, to be absolutely sure that a product plan will perfectly address a given market. New information is always coming in. It's everyone's job to be on the lookout for new disconfirming information at all times.

If you've spent months creating a particular plan, it only makes sense that you might become attached to it. You'll want to support it with as much evidence as you can find. Careful. This is when confirmation bias flourishes. Take care to wear your scientist's lab coat and be on the lookout for new disconfirming evidence.

We called this "getting married" to our plans. Resist! Don't be a bride or groom; be a scientist who's as happy to find evidence that disproves a theory as she is to find evidence that supports it. It's hard. The project you've been working on can feel like your baby. Why would you want to destroy it? The trick is to think of it not as your baby, but as a scientific theory that you'll be lauded for disproving as much as you would for proving. If the leaders of the group are on the lookout for such clear-eyed analysis and praise it, you're going to be fine.

This is the kind of thinking it takes to overcome confirmation bias.

Be fearless.

It's too easy to be deaf to what our customers are saying by operating from a place of fear, where retaining the status quo feels more comfortable than taking risks. You're just going to have to buck up and listen and, of course, take notes.

If you can't beat schemas, join them.

Do you know the assumptions in your schemas with regard to your customers or clients? Put together your best understanding of each type of customer's goals and challenges before the meeting.

Document and formally evolve your schemas with each customer alignment meeting. Then go into meetings and listen for comments that don't fall in line. Probe them and edit your premeeting schemas as needed.

Talk to many customers.

There's a tendency to believe that one customer represents all customers. While this simplifies the planning process, it can lead the team down the wrong path. On top of that, when people extrapolate from just one data point, these half-cocked understandings might be expressed with confidence and authority and have undue influence over product development. If your company is large enough, it's better to require that people attend a couple dozen customer alignment meetings and require them to contribute to the corporate schemas before materially participating in product-planning activities.

The Confirmation Bias Paradox

If you seek out disconfirming information, meet with customers who don't conform to your idea of what's typical, and hash out alternative theories of what customers are truly trying to do, you may find your head spinning from too much information. Your job may already be confusing enough, and here I am asking you to complicate things further by doubling down on understanding data that doesn't jibe with reality as you understand it. Sorry. Do it anyway. Here's why.

Imagine your boss asks for your report on what should be done to address a particular market. You're swimming in ambiguity and find it impossible to give clear direction. How do you tease out a simple course of action from this jumble of asterisked data points and tepid conclusions? Do you write up a memo that outlines various theories of what's going on? Probably not. That's the last thing your boss wants. Your boss is getting these reports from your colleagues as well and has to make sense of them all. Ambiguous reports from all sectors could drive your direct superior mad. You think you have it bad? Imagine your boss's dilemma. Indeed, this is why you've been asked to be decisive and keep your recommendations clear and simple. Do your best to present the clearest view of reality that you can, given the information you have. Give enough details to be useful, but also take care not to oversimplify in the other direction.

I've seen simplified assumptions in action. Sometimes they pan out; sometimes not so much. People who tended to rise up the ranks were often those who proved themselves to be decisive authorities on specific subjects. They would confidently declare what course of action needed to be pursued in very simple and easy-to-understand terms. When proven right, they would be promoted. Usually they were highly qualified and knowledgeable. However, sometimes these were the very same people who got married to their ideas. And why wouldn't they? They'd been rewarded handsomely for them.

The problem was that if they hadn't developed habits of checking their assumptions, or of seeking out disconfirming information, they could become blind to changes in the market. Thus oblivious, they got further married to their overly simplified ideas. Their bosses might love this because their reports and suggestions came across as clear and confident. However, in time, they became victims of their own confirmation bias, failing to rise up the ladder further.

This challenge where one strives to dig up disconfirming information, all while being expected to make decisive recommendations based on a sharp understanding of the situation, has a solution: talk to more customers. And then talk to still more customers. Keep talking to them and approach each one with a curious mind-set, with active listening questions at the ready. Prepare to be confused. Get comfortable with it. Be patient and wait for answers to emerge. Then be ready for those answers to be upturned by new information. This isn't a magic bullet. It takes time, patience, focus, and hard work. There's nothing like face time with customers to get a good sense of what they're trying to do.

Confirmation Bias Summary

Confirmation bias is a fundamental part of how our brains process information. However, it can be minimized. The first step is to acknowledge that it exists and understand how it works. Then review your premises and check the veracity of your observations and facts. Keep your eyes open for new information, especially anything that challenges conventional wisdom. Use the active listening skills described earlier. Think of plans dispassionately, as scientific theories rather than as precious possessions that would be painful to lose. Discuss your theories with colleagues and ask them to play devil's advocate; ask them how your theory might be wrong and how being wrong might affect future outcomes. Ask them for alternate descriptions of customer schemas. Lastly, use all the techniques listed above to cultivate such a mind-set. Most of all, make sure the data you're working from is as true as possible, by taking verbatim notes and asking active listening style questions.

This has been just a small chapter discussing the huge topic that is confirmation bias. To dive deeper, check out the book *Decisive* by Chip and Dan Heath.

CHAPTER TWELVE

People

"You have to get along with people, but you also have to recognize that the strength of a team is different people with different perspectives and different personalities." —Steve Case

MANAGING PERSONALITIES

THE RULE OF THUMB for working with customers of all types is to be straightforward and candid. Be clear about the agenda, set expectations, and start all customer alignment meetings using active listening skills to uncover customer goals and challenges. This advice stands no matter who your customer is. That said, you may find that different customer personality types or cultural backgrounds call for slightly different approaches.

First off, it pays to consult the sales team in a premeeting to assess what kind of customers are coming in and to determine whether the customer needs special handling. Maybe the customer has an extreme personality type or comes from a culture that's very different from yours.

The Greeks described four personality types or temperaments. In his book *Leadership from Within*, Peter Urs Bender expands these definitions by describing potential strengths and weaknesses of each temperament. Then he recommends how to engage with each type. Here's a brief summary: .

- Sanguine/Expressive: optimistic and social
- Choleric/Driver: short-tempered or irritable
- Melancholic/Analytical: soft-spoken or quiet
- Phlegmatic/Amiable: relaxed and peaceful

Sanguine or Expressive customers like to talk, and they typically enjoy the connecting process. Indeed, it's key that you connect with people of the expressive type before jumping into technical discussions or asking them to present their road map. Connect with them socially first, and they'll be more likely to open up later. One easy way to do this is to use an icebreaker during introductions. Icebreakers are off-topic, fun questions that prompt people to create answers that they themselves are exploring for the first time. Conversations stemming from icebreaker questions build connection and camaraderie. Icebreakers are discussed in further detail in Chapter Fourteen "Reviewing a Customer Alignment Meeting."

Allow plenty of time for people to get to know one another. Make sure the topic has nothing to do with the business at hand. The point of this exercise is to connect. If you have the time, meet the customer the day before for lunch. Try to identify common points of interest. This homophyly, otherwise known by the adage "birds of a feather flock together," can go a long way to making the expressive customer feel comfortable in the customer alignment meeting.

Choleric or driver customers loathe pointless chitchat. If you have a driver in your customer alignment meeting, be sure to get straight down to business. Within minutes of sitting down in the conference room, the group should do quick introductions (do not ask icebreaker questions with this personality type), review the agenda, and get on with the meeting.

If you can handle looking like an idiot, consider using a Cunningham bomb with a driver personality. This will immediately elicit detailed corrections. As always, use this technique sparingly because if a driver type comes to believe your team is stuffed with bumbling idiots, you'll find she wants to leave because you'll be considered a waste of her time.

I would normally argue against being argumentative with a customer. But if there's one time it may be acceptable, it's with a strong driver personality. Indeed, I've seen some customers who revel in debating. Consider calling one of the afternoon sessions "devil's advocate." In it, assign people to argue for and against some conventional wisdom. This will energize the driver. At the end of the session, ask whether anyone's beliefs changed. If a driver argues point B fervently, he still may believe point A. So make sure to confirm true beliefs before moving on. Don't worry: a driver will tell you if you ask.

Melancholic or analytical people are in their comfort zone when discussing facts. Above all, they value accuracy and precision. Uncomfortable with ambiguity, they can be reluctant to talk unless they are absolutely sure of themselves. Accuracy is prized. Mistakes are to be avoided. With analytical people, it's especially important to craft your questions in advance. Make them precise and fact-oriented. Avoid asking questions about how they feel and instead ask them questions about what is being planned and why. Also, when preparing your road map presentation, be sure to include as much data and analysis as you can. Once an analytical person sees that you speak her data-laden language, she may share more in subsequent sessions.

Cunningham bomb statements also work well with analytical people. Just be sure that the idiotic statement you make gets the facts, not the conclusions, wrong. They may not correct you on what they consider to be your own delusions. But they'll quickly correct the facts.

Phlegmatics or amiables can be tricky. People of this personality type go along to get along. They're supportive, diplomatic, and patient. These traits are their strengths and your problems. My former boss, Robert Blake, would describe talking with them as "pushing on a rope." They have no qualms if you hear the wrong message. Do not even think of using a Cunningham bomb with a phlegmatic/amiable. They'll happily let your question drop and step right over it as if it never exploded.

The key to working with an amiable personality is to be his partner in discovery. Amiables value cooperation and perseverance. After the initial uncovering session and after the road maps have been presented, call the subsequent sessions problem-solving or solution-finding sessions. Make it clear that you're on their team and your objective is to understand how you might contribute to their goals.

Whatever you do, do not be adversarial or confrontational. Amiables won't engage in an Oxford-style debate the way drivers will.

Conflicting Personality Types

If you have more than one customer with conflicting personality types, use your best judgment. Don't worry; your engagement doesn't need to be flawless. In my experience, most customers are a mix of the four personality types and, as a result, you needn't worry about engaging with them in any specific way. As long as you ask predominantly active listening questions followed by active listening after questions, you'll be fine.

That said, there's one scenario that calls for special care. If you get a vocal driver paired with a quiet amiable or analytical person in a meeting, then you'll need to go out of your way to give the quieter personality type a platform from which to talk. Use her name and ask her questions directly. Everyone on the team must be comfortable with silence as the more reserved personality might not respond enthusiastically or instantly. Give her space and time to answer, but don't take her silence as meaning she's got nothing to say. You may find the amiable or analytical customer has more useful information to share than the driver, but she needs time and space to think through her answers and you'll need to draw the answers out of her by addressing questions to her specifically. Take care to carve out portions of the conversation to get her input.

CULTURAL CONSIDERATIONS

Engaging with people from different cultures can be tricky. Assertiveness and emotional expressiveness can be interpreted in a variety of ways, depending on whom you're dealing with. I was lucky; I hosted many customer alignment meetings on my turf in San Jose, California. Most attendees were fully accustomed to American-style business meetings and had already taken steps toward my cultural norms. Even so, we attempted to be cognizant of whom we were meeting with and adapted as needed. You don't want to inadvertently offend anyone. Following are some cultural considerations to think about.

Language Considerations

You may meet with customers for whom the language to be spoken in the meeting is their second tongue. With such customers, you'll want to speak slowly and enunciate clearly. Depending on their competency level, there may be a bit of a delay between hearing your words and comprehending your meaning. Speaking slowly is considerate.

Second, avoid idioms. Phrases such as "in my neck of the woods" will add an unnecessary layer of complexity that requires decoding. A better phrase would be "where I am from."

Choose commonplace words. Colorful language has its place, but a customer alignment meeting with a nonnative speaker is not such a place. When a simple or frequently used word will communicate your message just as well as a complicated or arcane word, choose simplicity. For example, instead of saying you presented an oration, just say you spoke or gave a talk.

Cultural Norms

If you regularly meet with people from various cultures around the world, I urge you to read *The Culture Map: Breaking Through the Invisible Boundaries of Global Business* by Erin Meyer. This book is full of detailed and useful advice for engaging with people from just about every major culture.

She notes that Americans tend to value straightforward questions, reviewing action items, and clarifying positions. Indeed, much of the book you're reading right now is based on such American values. However, people from other cultures can interpret such gestures negatively. In a December 2015 *Harvard Business Review* piece by Meyer, "Getting to Si, Ja, Oui, Hai, and Da," a Saudi

Arabian businessman interprets a review of action items as an assault on his integrity. In anger, he bursts out, "You think I don't keep my promises?" The deal dies. Whoops.

When talking with people from foreign cultures, we can send unintended messages with seemingly innocuous comments. As Meyer observes, "What gets you to yes in one culture gets you to no in another." Tread cautiously and don't assume.

Confrontational versus Diplomatic or Obsequious Speech

People who like to argue tend to have thick skins. Meyer observes that in Russia, France, Israel, Germany, and the Netherlands, people tend to value confrontational speech, even if it's aggressive. Open disagreements are not only welcomed but seen as critical steps to coming to mutual understandings.

Other cultures that value moderately confrontational speech include Spain, Denmark, and Italy. People from these cultures may become suspicious if you seem too diplomatic or politically correct when you fail to argue a point. With people from these countries, you can let down your guard a bit and let yourself be a bit of a bulldog in a discussion.

Dropping a Cunningham bomb with conviction can work well in meetings with people who value confrontation, whether they be a driver type or simply from a more direct culture. It's an invitation to argue, and the chances are good that people from these cultures will immediately let you know how and why you are wrong. You must adopt a thick skin for this too!

On the other side of the spectrum are cultures that value diplomatic or even obsequious speech. In his book *Outliers*, Malcolm Gladwell gives a theory of an airplane crash on the north shore of Long Island. Gladwell largely blames a clash of cultures: one where direct speech is valued (New York) versus a culture of deferring to authority (Colombia). His theory is that the obsequious Columbian pilots deferred to the brash New York air traffic controllers before making sure the airport tower crew had all the necessary information. While Gladwell's theory of this specific case is contentious, the culture dynamic nonetheless illustrates how people from different cultures can fail to communicate due to their ideas about confrontation and proper protocol.

In cultures that value polite servile speech, aggressive confrontation is often interpreted as personal attack. With people from these cultures, it's useful to qualify disagreements, to state that you are not attacking. Invite these customers to explain more of their points of view in a gentle way. Ask them to explain what they mean rather than point out where they might have erred.

Displays of Emotion

Cultures can vary by how much they display emotion. When we consider this spectrum, two *Star Trek* species come to mind: Vulcans and Klingons. The Vulcans are the Germans, Dutch, and Danes. They engage in open disagreements willingly as long as the conversation remains dispassionate. Israelis, Russians, and French, on the other hand, are akin to Klingons. They, too, are open to disagreement but in a highly expressive manner. They can be argumentative to the point of hostility.

In my experience, Vulcans and Klingons are the easiest to work with because you generally know where they stand. Not so with people from cultures that consider confrontation to be offensive.

I worked in Southeast Asia for a few years. There, I found people tended to avoid confrontation and expressiveness. It left me wondering which way was up. As an American, I found it frustrating.

What I learned to do was invite my colleagues to share their ideas and express their opinions. I went out of my way to thank them for their efforts and was careful not to question their ideas in a wide forum. It felt like walking on eggshells, but that's what I had to do in order to make progress with my team.

Another group is made up of highly expressive yet non-confrontational cultures: Mexico, India, Saudi Arabia, and the Philippines. People from expressive and nonconfrontational cultures, says Meyer, "tend to disagree softly yet express emotions openly." So if you know you're working with a customer from such a culture, listen very carefully for complaints and disagreements. Probe for extra details. They won't tell you unless you ask.

Establish Trust

Meyer also describes how various cultures establish trust. Get this right because trust is the foundation for sharing open and honest information. There are two main ways people come to trust others: affectively and cognitively.

Affective trust is based on relationships, homophyly (or liking those with similar beliefs), and feelings of emotional connection and friendship. Affective trust is developed outside of the meeting room, during golf, dinner, or drinks. I remember stories of colleagues going to sauna houses in Finland and being plied with vodka all night. The next day at the meeting, they could barely function, but their Finnish counterparts were happy to work with them because they'd established an affective trust. Cultures that tend to require affective connections prior to engaging in business include Mexico, Turkey, China, Qatar, Finland, and Nigeria.

Conversely, cognitive trust comes from believing in another person's skills, accomplishments, or judgments. Americans and

Canadians tend to base trust in business exclusively on a cognitive basis. In fact, they tend to see affective trust as giving rise to potential conflict of interest. This disconnect is a reason North Americans might have difficulty doing business overseas. It's not that they necessarily avoid getting to know people, but they don't see such connections as prerequisites to business dealings.

The following are tactical suggestions for navigating these cultural differences, based on my own experience. This is hardly a complete list. It's simply a few tips you may find useful.

Business cards. With both Japanese and Chinese customers, learn how to exchange business cards! Customers expect a certain protocol that confers respect. If you want to be taken seriously, make sure you know how to exchange business cards with people from Asian cultures.

Here are the basics: offer your card with both hands, presenting the card like a gift. Similarly, when you receive a business card, receive it with both hands. Take ten to fifteen seconds to thoroughly read the card and mentally note the name and title. Read the card and commit the person's name to memory. You might use association (link their name to something you can remember, like Andy and the boy from the movie *Toy Story*). Or repetition, repeating their name back to them as you say, "Pleased to meet you, Mr. Smith" and then silently repeating "Mr. Smith" in your head as you look at Mr. Smith's face. Dale Carnegie's *How to Win Friends and Influence People* provides more on how to remember names.

Say the name out loud to confirm you are pronouncing it correctly. The key is to demonstrate you're interested in knowing about the person you're meeting. Next, place the card somewhere in a respectful manner. Don't shove it in your pocket or tuck it under other business cards. One idea is to place it on the table where you'll be sitting, perhaps above your notebook where you can view it during the meeting. Or come with a stylish business card holder and respectfully place it inside.

Punctuality, flexibility, and rigidity. In many cultures, being on time demonstrates respect. In others, meeting start times are merely suggestions. The best thing to do is be on time, but don't be rigid if others are not. This issue comes into play when you're hosting a customer alignment meeting. The agenda is crafted to allow for flexibility and moving topics around or adding discussions at the end. If your customer is from South America or Italy, he'll probably roll with that attitude easily. However, if your customer is from Northern Europe, deviating from the schedule may cause discomfort. In this case, review the agenda at the beginning of the meeting and get confirmation that any changes are acceptable.

Dress. Overdress for meetings. Wear suits or sophisticated business casual clothing. This is especially so for meeting with people from other cultures. On the other hand, I've encountered some customers, especially Silicon Valley engineers, who have little interest in talking to people in stiff suits. One memorable Silicon Valley luminary showed up to our meetings wearing Tigger T-shirts, board shorts, and flip-flops. While he talked to everyone, he seemed to prefer engaging with people dressed casually as he was. Even so, overdress unless the sales teams tell you otherwise. Take norms into account, but err on the side of overdressing.

Buyer Beware

In the end, if you know how to actively listen, that will go a long way to getting you on good terms with just about anyone from anywhere. Demonstrating a genuine interest in learning all you can about a customer's goals and challenges is the most important mind-set to cultivate.

Don't presume, however, based on the above that you can know someone's preference based on their cultural background alone. These are rules of thumb only. I've met people of contrary natures: punctual Italians and go-with-the-flow Japanese. Be aware of cultural preferences as a guideline, but work with individual customers to customize the day to them. Clear communication and continual checking-in is key.

CHAPTER THIRTEEN

Planning a Customer Alignment Meeting

"It's all in the preparation. A lot of things need to occur before you even start to cook."
—My mom, Marie Louise Montonye
    (who throws dinner parties that every guest enjoys)

N ow that mind-sets, roles, and tactics are all understood, let's delve into the mechanics of a well-run customer alignment meeting by specifically focusing on what the organizer and host need to tackle. In this chapter we will assume the CA meeting is an all-day affair. That said, you are welcome to adjust the agenda and times as makes sense for you.

ADVANCE PREPARATION

Customer alignment meetings don't start the day the customer walks in the front door. Planning begins days and even weeks before. There's a lot of preparation work to be done. Here's the master list of preparation tasks that must happen before the meeting.

1. Determine who will be invited from your company. Manage the head count.

2. Prepare the customer. Make sure she understands what is expected of her and get her input on the agenda.

3. Distribute and sign nondisclosure agreements with the customer so that attendees can be at liberty to speak somewhat freely.

4. Prepare a dossier of all pertinent information about the customer and the upcoming meeting. Distribute to internal attendees and interested parties.

5. Prepare a presentation of "What We Heard Last Time" that conveys exactly what the customers said in meetings. Present this twice: once to internal employees in the premeeting and once to the customers themselves in the CA meeting.

6. Book meetings on the calendars of all involved parties, including the premeeting, the individual sessions of the actual CA meeting, and internal follow-up meetings.

7. Assign roles to every attendee, including the scribes who will handle note-taking during various sessions and for various topics.

PREPARE THE CUSTOMER

Set expectations with the customer well in advance of the customer alignment meeting. Make sure they understand their role, the purpose, and what to expect from your team. Do your research. Gather information about your customers from the sales teams and from the customers. This will allow you to craft an appropriate draft agenda and invite the right internal attendees.

Here are some pointers when you are preparing the customer.

- Make sure all applicable nondisclosure agreements from your company and from the customer's company have been signed before the meeting happens. Without NDAs in place, your intellectual property is put at risk. I would advise against having CA meetings without properly executed NDAs. Contact your legal department to help with this.

- For some customers, especially those who are known to be litigious, work with your legal team to come up with a plan to make sure sensitive information isn't disclosed. (In my experience, it's rare to encounter customers who are overly litigious, but it's something to be aware of.)

- Work with the sales team to make sure the customer understands what the upcoming meeting is all about: a place to align road maps. Send the customer a questionnaire that does the following:

  - Sets expectations—that they will be presenting their goals and challenges

  - Asks questions that will guide the agenda and invitation list

The appendix on pages 255–256 includes a questionnaire you can use as a template. Send it to your customer a few weeks before the meeting. To increase the chances of receiving a reply to the questionnaire, the internal contact could set up an in-person meeting with the customer to walk him through the questions and to set expectations about the upcoming meeting. This could be someone on the sales team, the host, or both.

CREATE A CUSTOMER DOSSIER

Use the client's responses from the questionnaire or your prep meeting, as well as internal knowledge of the invited guests, to write a brief dossier that your teammates can read in preparation for the customer alignment meeting. The dossier should include the following:

- Names of the customers
- Their titles
- Their temperaments (expressive, driver, analytic, amiable)
- A brief history of their relationship with your company
- Any sensitive issues between your two companies
- Their influence and role within their company or industry
- The product they build and the market it serves
- Who their customers are
- The reason they use your product
- Any other relevant information about these customers

Store the dossier in a central location on the internal network and send a link to all internal meeting stakeholders. When you send out calendar invitations, make sure to include the link to the dossier.

CRAFT THE AGENDA

Craft a preliminary agenda using your best judgment, given what the customer wants to discuss balanced with the topics of interest among your colleagues. If the customer fails to reply to the questionnaire, work with the sales team to make the agenda.

Tactical Agenda Pointers

Start the agenda with a brief session specifically carved out for introductions. Then give the customer, XYZ Corp, a couple of hours to present their goals and challenges. Even if their presentation is only a few slides long, this will provide time for active listening questions. Remember, each ALQ can take anywhere from five to thirty minutes. Insert breaks every ninety minutes to two hours. Breaks should be long enough to make a quick call and go to the restroom.

Here's a sample agenda:

8:00 a.m.	Coffee, breakfast, introductions
8:30 a.m.	"What We Heard Last Time"
9:00 a.m.	XYZ Corp presents goals and challenges
10:45 a.m.	*Break*
11:00 a.m.	ABC Corp presents widget road map (lunch is brought in)
12:45 p.m.	*Break*
1:00 p.m.	Hardware discussion
2:15 p.m.	*Break*
2:30 p.m.	Software discussion
3:45 p.m.	*Break*
4:00 p.m.–5:00 p.m.	Open discussion and wrap-up

Remember, the key is to hear the customer's road map *first* and then dive into specific subjects. Having heard the customer's story, your team can focus on the topics that apply to the customer and skip over the bits that don't. The deep-dive subject matter expert-led discussions in the afternoon can be as short as thirty minutes or as long as a few hours.

Draft an agenda that is rooted in what you understand to be the customer's areas of interest and expertise. It doesn't have to be perfect. It's a starting point to review in the premeeting with your colleagues and adjust as needed.

You can call out more fine-grained sessions than this if necessary, but do so with caution. Shorter sessions can feel choppy and disjointed. The more fine-grained your schedule, the more you'll find you need to ask people to move on from the current discussion to the next. That can be counterproductive. You're tacitly communicating that sticking to the agenda is more important than open, honest, thorough conversation. This is the opposite of what a customer alignment meeting should be. The agenda should facilitate talking points, not dictate them.

An alternative is to book sessions that are two to three hours each. Then call out subtopics within those. The subtopics will serve as reminders to make sure you discuss everything the customers care about, without being too rigid.

There's another problem with an agenda that's too granular: it sends the message that it's acceptable for people to come and go every half hour. This can be disruptive. It impedes free and forthright exchanges of ideas because it can feel like a revolving door of new faces.

Again, make sure the agenda is crafted according to the customer's interests. If it's based on your self-interests, you risk failing to connect with your customers at all. It can be disastrous. Second, break the agenda into high-level topic sessions. An excessively granular agenda might be too difficult to follow and may include topics that the customers didn't want to discuss.

A CA meeting is not a sales meeting, nor is it a training session. Do not schedule sessions that serve to promote your latest services or provide training on your latest products. If you feel you need to pack the agenda with sessions that educate the customer on what you're currently rolling out to the market, then delay the meeting until after those presentations have been provided in a separate forum.

Of paramount importance is that every session on the agenda addresses the customer's interest.

WHO TO INVITE FROM THE CUSTOMER COMPANY

In Chapter Two: "Roles and Responsibilities," we discussed who to invite from customer companies. Long story short: invite Professors, not Gilligans. Ideal customers are people who possess the following knowledge, skills, and influence:

- They know their products.
- They know their markets.
- They understand why and how they use your company's products.
- They influence their company's direction and road maps.

WHO TO INVITE FROM THE HOST COMPANY

Attendees from the host company should be subject matter experts who not only demonstrate credibility but who also know how to actively listen. If they read this book and demonstrate the ability to use the skills discussed herein, then they pass the first hurdle. It'll be up to the meeting organizer and host to determine who to invite beyond that. If the customer is pushing the boundaries on IO technologies, then invite the resident expert or developer for IO technologies.

Attendees from your company might be product planners, engineers, direct sales staff, and executives. There should be a good reason for each person to be present in the customer alignment meeting. Every person should bring something of value.

An executive sponsor who listens and uses restatement to confirm his understanding during the meeting will convey not only that the customer is important to your company but also that they are being heard, even at the highest levels. This can motivate the customer to talk more.

A product planner who can competently navigate listening, questioning, understanding, and presenting a road map is key to the meeting.

An SME from engineering who can talk shop with the customer will convey that the customer's comments will not be lost on the crowd. The customer will know that there is core expertise in the room. As such, the customer may be nudged to be forthright and discuss a topic in greater depth than he otherwise would.

BOOK THE MEETINGS

Here's an overview of how we booked our customer alignment meetings. Adjust according to your processes as needed.

Book a premeeting.

This should be at least an hour long, but if you can, schedule ninety minutes. Invite everyone involved with the customer alignment meeting: subject matter experts, presenters, executive sponsors, direct sales teams—especially them. Sales teams often know the most about the customer, and they'll be the stars of the premeeting. (I'm assuming here that you have a direct sales force that is employed by your company. If this is not the case, I strongly urge you to seriously consider whether you want to pull in employees from other companies. They might have different objectives from yours. In my experience, meetings with external sales forces should be carved out separately.)

Invite those not able to attend the meeting to still contribute to the premeeting.

Book the customer alignment meeting according to the draft agenda.

I found that the best way to manage the actual customer alignment meeting was to book multiple sessions rather than one long meeting that blocked everyone's calendar for the entire day. That also allowed me to manage the head count, as I could invite only the people I wanted at each session. That said, most attendees should be present when the customer presents her goals and challenges in the initial uncovering session.

A CA meeting calendar might look like the following, where five separate meetings are booked back-to-back in the same conference room (breaks are removed for now):

8:00 a.m.–9:00 a.m.	Coffee, breakfast, introductions, "What We Heard Last Time"
9:00 a.m.–11:00 a.m.	XYZ Corp presents goals and challenges
11:00 a.m.–1:00 p.m.	ABC Corp presents widget road map (lunch is brought in)
1:00 p.m.–2:30 p.m.	Hardware discussion
2:30 p.m.–4:00 p.m.	Software discussion
4:00 p.m.–5:00 p.m.	Open discussion and wrap-up

Consider booking the conference room for the entire day in one monolithic meeting block, but don't add attendees to this booking. This will reserve the room and keep people from trying to use the room before or after your scheduled meeting times and allow you to set up in peace. It also gives you the option to keep talking at the end of the meeting if everyone is so inclined.

Book the follow-up meeting.

Put the follow-up meeting on everyone's calendars *ASAP*, even before you hold the premeeting. If you leave this as an afterthought, follow-up may never happen. As much as people may complain about too many meetings, hold the follow-up meeting anyway and book it for ninety minutes. If you're done in sixty, great! However, the follow-up meeting is where the team digests what they heard. It's where they come to agreement on what the main takeaways were and what actions should be taken. It's where you collectively develop the corporate schema for this one specific customer. You don't want to rush this process. If you're not willing to hold a follow-up meeting, I would suggest closing this book and not inviting customers in for alignment meetings at all. What's the point in spending the entire day with a customer if you're not going to make sense of what you learned?

MATERIALS FOR THE PREMEETING

Bring the customer dossier and the preliminary agenda to the premeeting for review. If applicable, prepare and bring along a presentation that details what was learned the last time the customer visited.

What We Heard Last Time

If you've invited a customer who has attended a customer alignment meeting in the past, then prepare a short presentation titled something like "What We Heard Last Time." Include a handful of verbatim comments the customer made in the previous CA meeting, drawn from the notes. Include the conclusions discussed at the end of the meeting. If you can report any relevant internal developments that have since occurred, dedicate a slide to each one so you can bring the customer up to speed. Don't worry, not every comment they made in the previous meeting needs to be followed up on or reported back.

This will be delivered after introductions but before the customer's presentation. It's a sophisticated long-play in terms of using restatement to confirm understanding. Make the slides heavy on what the customer told you last time, and as verbatim as possible, just as you would do when using restatement to check for understanding during a live active listening question session.

There may be some items in the presentation that your company has taken action on or used in their developments in some way. Briefly mention or note these activities in the slides and be clear that you can get into details later in the day. Whatever you do, don't pander. Don't make it sound like you took their feedback, turned around, and began handcrafting a product just for this client, unless it's true. If you catch yourself exaggerating your efforts, back it up and report just the facts.

All this material (the dossier, the presentation, the agenda, and the "What We Heard Last Time" presentation) will be edited and improved during the premeeting. Do your best to collect as much information as you can and take an honest stab at the agenda. If you're able to pull together 80 percent of the information your company has on the customer, you're doing great. This information will serve as starting points for discussion in the team's premeeting. It needn't be perfect. It does, however, need to largely represent the topics to be discussed and contain pertinent information. The more you prepare, the more efficiently and quickly you can run the premeeting.

HOLD THE INTERNAL PREMEETING

Got all that material together? Good. You should hold internal premeetings three to five days prior to every customer alignment meeting. In the premeeting, the host and meeting organizer lead the following discussions:

- **Review the goal of a customer alignment meeting.** Remind everyone that the team will be working together to use active listening techniques in order to uncover the customer's future goals and challenges.

- **Brief the team** about the customer company's background, product, and market, using the dossier that was prepared earlier. Review any topics or current issues that the customer might be sensitive to.

- **Discuss the temperaments of the customers** and whether any special engagement techniques are required. Such tips can be found in chapter twelve, entitled "People." This chapter provides advice for managing meetings that include attendees with strong temperaments or come from cultures with diverse norms.

- **Agree on dress code.** Some meetings call for suits and others call for relaxed business casual.

- **Review topics** that will be discussed in depth as well as relevant history with this customer on each topic.

- **Review the "What We Heard Last Time" presentation.** Incorporate feedback from the team.

- **Finalize the agenda**. Review goals, roles, and responsibilities for each session.

- **Identify hosts, presenters, notetakers, and subject matter experts for each session.** Make sure everyone understands their particular role in each session, as this can change throughout the day. People need to be clear about what they are responsible for. I cannot stress this enough. Don't leave anything to chance when it comes to roles and responsibilities. One person might be a scribe in one session and then an SME in the next. They need to know what they're responsible for and when.

- **Discuss how to demonstrate credibility**, identifying who should say what. (It's usually briefly done during introductions.)

- **Obtain agreement that everyone will submit verbatim notes within a day** after the meeting concludes and that they'll attend the postmeeting.

- **Review presentation materials** that are to be shown to the customers. Make sure the presentation slides are about the company's future road map and don't sell the customer on current products. Slides should only be presented if they are designed to spur discussion. By no means are slides required for every session. Consider leading uncovering sessions at the whiteboard with nothing but a dry erase marker and eraser.

- **Develop questions** to be asked during each session. Keep in mind that these questions may or may not be asked in the CA meeting. Often only a portion of the questions get asked due to time constraints or to the questions not fitting into the discussion. Remind people that's okay.

- **Practice alignment skills.** Pick a skill and rehearse it. For example, you might have a few team members ask active listening questions and follow up with active listening after questions, with a special focus on using restatement.

- **Reconfirm scribes.** Before anyone leaves the room, make sure every scribe understands which session or topic they'll be recording.

CHAPTER FOURTEEN

Reviewing a Customer Alignment Meeting

"If we wait until we're ready, we'll be waiting for the rest of our lives." —Lemony Snicket

BEFORE THE CUSTOMER ARRIVES

IT'S SHOWTIME. You've held your premeeting, the customer is soon to arrive, and you're standing alone in the conference room. You've checked that all the logistical details, like catering and seating, have been seen to. Now, it's time to do one simple thing to make the customer alignment meeting run smoothly.

Write the agenda on a whiteboard or easel in the front of the room so that everyone can see it throughout the meeting.

Do yourself a favor: write in large print so people on the opposite side of the room can read it. Post the agenda where it's visible to every seat for the course of the entire meeting. In other words, it needs to be large, persistent, physical, and highly visible.

A large permanent agenda is an indispensable meeting management aid. During introductions, you can review the agenda and adjust it if necessary. During the meeting, it will serve as a reference that all attendees can use to orient themselves within the day, be they sitting around the table or walking in the room between sessions. The host also can use it as a tool to manage the discussion. He can point out the agenda and bring the conversation back to the topic at hand. Conversely, if the discussion is off-topic but fruitful, the host can edit the agenda to strike other topics or extend the session. He can do this all while people continue the conversation.

This may seem like a minor tactic, but in my experience, having a large, visible, and permanent agenda freed me to focus on the discussion because it allowed people to serve themselves agenda information without interrupting me.

Alternatives that I've seen are worthless. Putting the agenda in a slide deck is fine at the beginning of the meeting, but then the slide disappears as soon as the next presentation is loaded. Printing the agenda in handouts is slightly better, but then you have multiple copies and if you make adjustments midmeeting, there's no guarantee that everyone will stay up-to-date with the changes.

Trust me on this: write the agenda in a visible and persistent location in the conference room. For each agenda item or session, note the times, topic of discussion, name of the presenter/discussion leader, and name of the notetaker or scribe. For example:

8:30 a.m.	Coffee and breakfast
8:45 a.m.	Introductions
9:00 a.m.–10:45 a.m.	XYZ Corp presents goals and challenges (<customer name>; notes: Cheryl and Samir)
10:45 a.m.	*Break*
11:00 a.m.	ABC Corp road map (Gary; notes: Tom)

12:00 p.m.	Lunch brought in, continue discussion
12:45 p.m.	*Break*
1:00 p.m.–2:15 p.m.	Hardware discussion (Amy; notes: Bob)
2:15 p.m.	*Break*
2:30 p.m.–4:00 p.m.	Software discussion (Bob; notes: Amy)
4 :00 p.m.	*Break*
4:15 p.m.–5:00 p.m.	Open discussion and wrap-up (Tom; notes: Gary)

This agenda calls out start times, end times, breaks, discussion leaders, notetakers, and even catering. It may feel odd to write down the names of the notetakers, but it accomplishes two things. For one, it reminds the official scribes that they signed up for taking notes. There's no way Bob can say "I didn't know I was the notetaker" when his name is clearly written on the agenda. Second, it conveys to the customer that you care about capturing the story they tell you. It tells them they matter.

SETTLING IN

When Customers Arrive

Invite the customers to sit near a whiteboard, so they will be more inclined to make use of it to brainstorm ideas during the discussion. Offer them coffee, tea, or whatever catering has been arranged. Provide them with Wi-Fi passwords and instructions for getting to the bathroom.

A Sincere Thank-You

The host should kick off the meeting by thanking the customers for taking the time to meet. Optionally, invite an executive to deliver a prepared statement of appreciation and partnership. Use your best judgment here. It can come off as overkill or it can be a winning gesture, depending upon the temperaments of your customers. Whether you take thirty seconds to say thanks for your time or five minutes for an executive to deliver a heartfelt message, a clear delivery of gratitude should be made, no matter what. After all, these customers are taking time out of their busy schedules to talk with you and the rest of the team. Make sure they know you appreciate it.

Review the agenda.

Line item by line item, including breaks, review the agenda with everyone in attendance. Let the customers know that the agenda is a guideline to support the discussion and can be adjusted as needed. Ask the customers if anything is missing or whether they'd like to make adjustments. Once the agenda is agreed to, move on to introductions.

INTRODUCTIONS

Don't assume everyone knows one another. Carve out ten to twenty minutes to do a formal round of introductions. In this part of the meeting, attendees will have the opportunity to briefly demonstrate their credibility and express what they hope to get out of the meeting.

My colleague, Martin Lee, taught me the following phrase to use to kick off introductions. It worked like magic, and I thank him for his suggestion. Say something like "Before we begin, let's introduce ourselves. We'll go around the table and, one at a time, say who you are, what you work on, and what you'd like to get out of the meeting." As you say this, write the three points on a whiteboard:

- Who you are

- What you work on

- What you hope to get out of the meeting

I start with myself and invite the person to my right or left to go next. If establishing credibility isn't required, then I keep it simple, saying something like "My name is Laura. I work in the product-planning department. I'm responsible for understanding the memory needs of our customers so that we might develop products that incorporate the right memory technologies. I hope to gain an understanding of your company's goals and challenges so that we might align our road maps in an informed way going forward."

Now, on the other hand, if we decided in the premeeting that we need to establish some credibility with the customers, I might say something that's a little more long-winded, such as "My name is Laura Reese. I work in the product-planning department. I'm responsible for understanding the internal memory and external memory needs of our top customers so that we might develop products that incorporate the right memory technologies. A recent project was planning stacked die products along with my colleague here, Samir. Today I hope to gain an understanding of XYZ Corp's goals so that we can understand what may be appropriate to help meet those goals. More broadly, I'm hoping to learn your goals and challenges so that we might better align our broader road maps in an informed way going forward." Everyone goes around the room and gives their answers to each of the three items in similar fashion.

Consider using icebreakers during the introduction.

An icebreaker is an off-topic, thought-provoking question that fosters personal connections. They can mix the serious with the silly and are easily found online. Consider your crowd and pick a question that will not only be unexpected but will foster lively story-telling. What's nice about icebreakers is that they inspire answers that people must come up with on the fly, rather than canned answers such as what a person does for a living.

Icebreakers shake up things by diverting the discussion away from serious business for a few minutes. They provide a platform for every attendee to display their personalities to whatever degree they choose. People on the aligning team might tell a story that shows vulnerability, thereby demonstrating to the customers that this customer alignment meeting is a safe place. If you have difficulty coming up with a good icebreaking question on your own, find a suitable-for-work version online. If you are in doubt about the appropriateness of an icebreaker exercise, err on the side of caution. An example might be asking, "What's one of your favorite movies and why?" It's not rocket science.

Last, if you choose to use icebreakers, be sure to add adequate time to the introductions section of the agenda. Budget an extra three to five minutes per attendee.

A FORUM FOR THE CURIOUS

Before anyone presents slides or asks questions, take a minute to remind the attendees that the purpose of the meeting is to swap road maps. By the end of the meeting, every attendee on the aligning team should have a working knowledge of what the customer is trying to do. Conversely, the customer should have a good idea of what plans and open decisions lie ahead for your products and services under development.

Depending on the crowd, you could explicitly remind everyone that this means they try to see the world from the other point of view, putting aside what they think they know, gathering their courage, and asking questions for the express purpose of gaining knowledge about each other's motivations and perspectives. Take risks, realizing that failure can lead to creativity and new ideas.

Everyone comes to the table with a different set of experiences and training, so it's possible that some people may ask questions that seem naive. Try to answer them honestly and thoroughly, even if you think everyone should know the answer. Sometimes covering the basics sparks real insights into what's really going on.

STUFF YOU NEED TO FIGURE OUT ON YOUR OWN

Before we get into the details of how to run an effective customer alignment meeting, I want to call out specific details that are important for you to get right.

Basic Housekeeping Tasks and Meeting Logistics

I'm assuming you and your organization can handle the basic housekeeping required for running a professional meeting. Even if I don't discuss them directly, they still are supremely important. A few examples:

- Print name badges ahead of time.
- Provide Wi-Fi credentials and passwords.
- Arrange for travel and parking.

- Order appropriate catering.

- Book conference rooms.

- Present thoughtful gifts.

- Provide adequate seating.

- Provide appropriate office supplies, such as notepads, pens, dry erase markers, paper easels, laser pointers, etc.

- Do anything else to make your customers feel welcome and special.

These details are critical, and I'll leave it to you to make them happen. The main point is to execute on the small things that leave your customers feeling like they are meeting with professionals who genuinely care about their experience and appreciate their time. Whatever you need to do to accomplish this, do it. Assign a specific person to take care of these items and establish standard procedures if you must. My point: don't take my lack of commentary on this stuff to mean it's not important. Indeed, if you can't get these things right, don't bother holding the customer alignment meeting.

Identify customer companies to target.

I'm assuming that your team is capable of identifying which companies and divisions of said companies to invite in for a customer alignment meeting. After all, you know your business better than I do. It's up to you to know whom you want to align with. That said, I have provided tips for inviting the right people from within those groups in chapters three and thirteen. One thing to consider is sample bias. Be sure you're talking to enough customers within each market segment to guarantee you're getting a wide enough view.

Size and segment your end markets.

This is a tactical book. I have strong opinions on how to size and segment markets. Even so, I'm going to leave that to you. This book focuses on how to run customer alignment meetings so that you get as much accurate information as possible from one customer company at a time. How you put that story together and how you judge the relative importance of information from one meeting to another is up to you.

IT Infrastructure

Hoo-boy! Building a notes repository sounds like a straightforward project. In my experience, however, it was challenging. I offer here some of the lessons learned so that when you look to buy or build a notes repository, you can take these requirements into account.

Permissions. Customer data is sensitive. Getting the permissions right is critical. There's raw data, metadata, and then all that needs to be tied into the sales team's customer relationship management databases. You need data to be accessible to the right people, but you can't make it freely available to everyone. Furthermore, people who have access also must receive training so that they understand how to handle customer-sensitive data, such as how to refer to it in reports or external documentation.

Usability. People who work with the data need to be able to easily generate reports, receive relevant notifications, and be able to see meetings through their calendar. When they're searching for answers, the database search function must be thorough and user-friendly.

Getting people to use the IT. There's a point you need to get to where enough people are using the system and putting data into it, making it useful to everyone.

Subject matter experts and presenters need to understand that they are required to submit verbatim notes to the centralized repository. A way of ensuring success is to make sure everyone on the uncovering team understands specifically the notes they're responsible for as well as their due date.

My Experience with IT Infrastructure

It took a few years to get our repository to a place where it was usable and useful. First, I battled old-timers who couldn't see why e-mailing attendees the notes after a meeting wasn't the best solution. "Uh, dude, I can't search *your* in-box. Besides, even if I could, the results would be a nightmare to sort through."

Next, I worked with two engineers from a start-up to develop a beta product around our needs. It fell apart under the complexity. But the experience gave me a better idea of what could be workable.

Then I worked with our IT department to implement a database in our existing customer relationship management, but the interface was awkward for end users and they protested using it. We designed around the graphical user interface limitations and came up with keyboard shortcuts that not only made it usable but also was straightforward and serviceable. People in my immediate group entered actual customer notes into the system. The back end was magical. The database allowed for categorizing notes and tagging various passages, so we were able to generate effective reports. Then, *whammo!* We were forced to update the customer relationship databases, which killed the keyboard shortcuts and did weird things to the database queries. Now people had to click through multiple drop-down menus and panels to accomplish tasks that previously had been done with a single keyboard command. In the end, we had to abandon it.

Next, I wrote a lightweight database using MySQL with ASP pages. That worked marginally well for storing customer alignment meeting logistics and data, but it was a nonsanctioned side project that I developed personally so we got what we paid for. I had other jobs to do. Abandoned.

We tried SharePoint, in its many different alpha and beta incarnations. It wasn't a good fit. Abandoned.

We tried to use some technology that bolted on to our e-mail system. As is typical with so many of these efforts, the technology was touted as if it was going to solve all problems. Turned out, not so much. Data syncing bogged it down. Abandoned.

We tried a new online system that was akin to Facebook. The permissions and fit were poor for our needs.

At last, we put together a cross-functional task force to look at the problem with fresh eyes and propose a properly resourced solution. We evaluated various customer relationship management databases as well as other platforms. We came up with a bit of a hodgepodge solution, but it was workable.

This topic could merit an entire book on its own. Indeed, our cross-functional team wrote an extensively researched internal paper on the subject, in the hopes of finding a better solution. For now, I'm conveniently hereby declaring that data storage and IT architecture are beyond the scope of this book. I'll leave it to you. My advice would be to make the project a high-priority effort and get high-level buy-in for providing adequate resources at the outset. Properly scope the project straight-away and obtain plenty of resources from your IT department. In other words, get top management behind you and ask for more resources than you think you'll need. Because you'll need them.

WHAT WE HEARD LAST TIME

"What We Heard Last Time" is a presentation that is given to returning customers. It specifically focuses on what that particular customer told you in the previous meeting and not much more. Present "What We Heard Last Time" after introductions and before the customer's presentation. *Keep it brief.* When you present "What We Heard Last Time," you are reminding the customer that you care and that you listened in the last meeting.

You may find the customers laugh at something they said previously, and you can be sure they'll fill you in on developments since then. Don't squander this opportunity. Present what you heard last time and prime your customer to open up.

Be careful, however. Make sure you only present what the customer actually told you. Present verbatim comments and brief factual developments since the last meeting. If you share your internal conclusions, you may open yourself up to a battle. On one hand, you might think this a good thing because the customer would confirm or contradict your conclusions. The problem is it could derail the conversation. The customer doesn't know all your internal trade-offs, goals, and challenges. Some of your conclusions from the previous meeting—about whether or not to develop a new technology, for example—might make sense in the context of all the customer information you have but make no sense when considering this one customer. No, it's better they argue with their own words and then uncover their updated story about their goals and challenges. Later in the day you can discuss internal conversations that happened in the interim but only after you've updated your understanding of their story.

XYZ CORP PRESENTS GOALS AND CHALLENGES

Everyone has settled in and introductions have been made. Now is the time to put your active listening skills to work. So get ready to sit down, listen, and shut up. This portion of the meeting is where your customer, XYZ Corp, presents its goals and challenges. Your customer is doing the talking, not you. Your role is to listen and learn. Put aside your agenda, put aside your questions, and listen. Remember that meditation exercise from chapter nine where you note discursive thoughts, affix them to a balloon, and let them go? Now's the time to practice this so that your mind is clear to hear what's said.

Let the meeting host lead the open-ended questioning. The first questions should ask about the customer's goals and challenges and absolutely should not lead the customer into pet topics. You can help the team by restating what you heard, when appropriate, and asking follow-up questions such as "What else?" or "Anything else?" Keep going with a single line of questioning until the customer says she's done answering.

As the session progresses, you, too, can ask questions. Before you do, however, please be mindful that you must limit yourself to asking active listening questions. When you ask your questions, expect your teammates to help get the full answer by using follow-up questions, just as you did for them. Keep going until . . . that's right! . . . until the customer says she's fully answered the question.

This is the session where your aligning skills matter the most. It's where everyone works together for the same purpose: to uncover the customer's goals and challenges. Do everything you can to support this effort.

Once you've unearthed all the customer's goals and challenges, you are set for success. In subsequent sections, when you present your road map or topic of interest, you can use the information you learned in this session to focus on the topics that are relevant for this customer and skim over topics that aren't.

ABC CORP PRESENTS WIDGET ROAD MAP

This session is where your company presents your road map. What you present is up to you. Perhaps you show a suite of services your law firm intends to offer, discuss a diagram of a widget under development, or display ten slides of open questions you're striving to answer. Any of those can work, as long as you let the customer guide the discussion.

Use what you learned during the XYZ Corp presentation to guide your road map presentation.

The critical thing here is to refer to what you learned about XYZ Corp's goals and challenges. Use that information to adjust your road map presentation. Spend time on topics that the customers can provide feedback on and simply note items that likely don't apply. Pay attention to the customer and his level of interest. Don't present a topic you care about for an hour when the customer clearly isn't interested in hearing about it. Conversely, don't assume a customer won't be interested in a topic he hasn't brought up already.

Here's a neat trick for figuring out whether a topic matters to a customer: *Ask her!*

Continually check in with the customer.

This advice may seem obvious. It is obvious. But I've seen many people bungle their road map presentations by not realizing they can ask the customer what to focus on. If you're not sure whether to talk about a topic in-depth, ask the customer, "Would you like me to elaborate on this?" Or if you think a topic is not of interest for the customer, ask him something like "I suspect this technology doesn't apply to your situation. Would you like me to skip over it?"

This was covered in chapters seven and eight under the advice "The Art of Questioning." It's as if a one-way mirror exists between the presenter and the audience, where the presenter doesn't see the audience and only hears herself. She doesn't realize she has an option to interact with the people at the table. It doesn't occur to her that she can ask them which points to focus on and which slides to skip.

If you have trouble interacting with your audience while presenting, take a presentation training class. Audience interaction and continual checking in are critical when you present any topic in a customer alignment meeting. When you're unsure whether a topic matters to a customer, simply ask. Don't worry. They won't be offended. More likely, they'll be relieved.

LUNCH

You only have so much time in the day, so you might make lunch a working one. You can time it so that lunch is brought into the conference room during your road map presentation to the customer. That way, the customers don't feel like they have to talk; they can listen and eat. They spent the morning explaining in detail their road maps. By lunch they're tired. This is their chance to sit back, relax, and be presented to. Don't worry. They can still engage in dialogue, and you can ask them questions during this session—just not when their mouths are full.

Another option is to use lunch as a leg-stretcher. If you have a corporate dining room, move the meeting to that. Don't schedule any topics and simply let people chat. Consider incorporating a tour of the facilities after lunch, if there's anything of interest to see at your location.

TOPIC SESSIONS

After road maps have been presented—first the customer's, then yours—it's time for deep-dive discussions.

Remember that questionnaire you asked the customer to fill out in preparation for the customer alignment meeting? If it indicated that your visitor wanted to discuss specific details, now is the time. Bring in the team responsible for that specific subject and let them have at it.

Start by restating the goals and challenges the customer described earlier that have to do with this topic. For example, if the topic is software tools, restate comments the customer made about software.

Remember how I asked you to be patient at the beginning of the meeting and hold on to all those burning questions? Well, now that you know the customer's story, now is the time to go ahead and ask specific, open-ended questions about your topic of interest. Keep in mind that it's okay for the customer to say, "I don't know." Use what you know about their goals and challenges to parse through your questions and ask the ones that make sense.

Use active listening techniques. They'll serve you well here. But don't get too hung up. The topic sessions are for back-and-forth talking. They can be informal, depending on the crowd. If a rapport has developed, you can even challenge the customer on some of her assumptions. Don't be a jerk, of course, but if you honestly don't understand how she's come to some conclusions, ask questions that get you to that understanding. Just be aware that if she doesn't know, then you need to stop.

In my experience, these sessions vary wildly, depending on the topic and the attendees. The best advice I can give you is to make sure that everyone on your team is well-versed in the arts of crafting active listening questions, taking notes, and listening. Furthermore, make sure they're aware of any hot-button topics, *before* they come to the CA meeting. For example, if the customer is still waiting for engineering samples or hasn't received an answer on a question about your services, avoid making statements such as "Our company prides itself on fast response times and delivering products ahead of schedule." That'll go over like the Hindenburg.

Beyond that, loosen up. It's a conversation. Discuss what the customer is trying to achieve and the obstacles in the way. Keep everything in the context of the customer's reality and viewpoint. That said, this is the session where you can openly brainstorm various solutions or offer ideas and get feedback on which options would work best for the customer and why. Ask trade-off questions if you're not clear on the relative importance of feature requests. While those kinds of questions are self-centered and inappropriate during the initial uncovering session, they are completely appropriate, in moderation, during the topic deep dives.

During topic sessions, your enthusiasm may expand as you realize you're with a customer who can talk shop about the technology you work on. This is the time to remember Epictetus's observation that we have two ears and one mouth for a reason. Continue to ask ALQs and keep the story about the customer's experience for the majority of the conversation.

Remember to pay attention to body language and the engagement level of the customer. If you find the customer is being less than forthright, then double back. Ask yourself, Have you gone overboard in talking about your own problems or solutions? Are you discussing a subject he has little interest in? If you're not sure what's going on, check in with the customer. State your observations and ask them what's on their mind. Go back to asking more questions about their perspective in order to bring the conversation back to them.

OPEN DISCUSSION AND WRAP-UP

Reserve at least a half hour at the end of the day for open discussions. During the course of the meeting, the team may discover the customer can talk about an important topic that hadn't been expected. Behind the scenes, the host can invite appropriate attendees to come in during this final open session to drill down into details. In my experience, we made use of the open session maybe a third of the time. When we did, it usually resulted in very frank and useful conversations. The customers appreciated our flexibility and willingness to bring in engineers and experts as needed.

More times than not, however, our original agenda covered all relevant topics and the final session was used as a time buffer into which we could expand previous sessions.

Wrap-up

The last session is the wrap-up. Allow at least a half hour to close out the meeting properly.

When wrapping up the meeting, the host asks a simple question: "Think back on the day. If we could only remember five bits of information from our meeting today, what would you have us remember?"

This is where everyone needs to be comfortable with silence and let the customers think. They'll reply with a couple obvious answers. Write them on the whiteboard.

Are you done? Hardly. It's time to follow up. Ask, "Anything else?"

That's right. This is the final active listening question of the day. Make it count. Even though you asked for five things, let the customers answer until they're done. Consider writing each item on a whiteboard and let them tell you how to order the comments in terms of importance. Stop when they say they're done.

Next, each of the scribes or session leaders can restate themes and comments they'd heard during various sessions. This can help the customer remember some items he may have forgotten for that final list of five things. Adjust the list on the whiteboard as directed.

The next step is tactical. Review action items that were captured during the day. If your team succeeded in acting like Teflon, there should be very few. In any case, now is the time to review the actions and let the customer correct the list.

Set expectations.

Explain what the customer can expect next: The host will collect notes from all the attendees and will e-mail a copy within one week. Explain to the customer that the team will appreciate his reading through the notes and letting them know of any corrections or additional information that may have been missed.

Schedule the next meeting.

Explain that aligning is an ongoing process. One-off meetings are great, but it's better to meet regularly. Ask when the customer would like to meet again. Given the nature of our product design cycles, I usually suggested twelve to eighteen months. Depending on your product schedule, those phases may vary. Work with your customer, during the wrap-up, to come to an agreement on when to meet next. It needn't be a specific date but could be a target month or quarter.

Say thank you.

Finally, thank the customer for her time, effort, stamina, etc. If you and the sales team want to take her to dinner, by all means do that. It's up to you.

To reiterate, make sure to schedule a half hour or more for wrapping up. It's better to schedule too much time and wrap up early than to not schedule enough and rush the ending.

A Note for Scribes

Scribes are probably exhausted from sitting in a meeting and taking notes. Nevertheless, a best practice is for scribes to type up (and clean up) notes immediately after the meeting. Make sure the notes are complete and as verbatim as possible. Polishing the spelling and grammar can wait until the next day, but don't wait until the next day to record any comments or memories that are fresh in mind as the meeting closes. Get them all recorded before you go home.

CHAPTER FIFTEEN

The Day after a Customer Alignment Meeting

"Just pick away at it. One thing at a time."
—My dad, Captain James T. Montonye

SCRIBES

REMEMBER THE NOTE-TAKING SKILLS? Now is the time for them to shine. The day after the customer alignment meeting, every scribe is expected to submit cleaned-up and verbatim notes into the system. This may seem like a tight turnaround time, but it's critical. Our brains are terrible at retaining information with high fidelity. The longer we wait to tidy up notes and the more people we talk to between the meeting and meeting summary, the less reliable our memories become.

Notes must be in the system within one business day of the meeting—two at the latest. By filing notes quickly, you increase data retention all while helping the host pull together the meeting summary quickly. The host will take your notes and collate them into one document along with everyone else's notes. From that, they'll write up the meeting summary that will be sent to the customer and presented in the internal postmeeting. It's crucial you get your notes to the host as soon as possible.

CREATE THE CUSTOMER ALIGNMENT SUMMARY DOCUMENT

When the host summarizes the meeting, he can start with the dossier from the premeeting. It already contains most of the customer-specific information. All that needs to be done is to adjust it to reflect newly learned information and add the main takeaways from the customer alignment meeting. And that's easy, because the main takeaways were learned during the wrap-up session. Remember that final active listening question: "What five things would you have us remember?" The answer is all you need. Between that and the updated dossier, you have the meeting summary.

Next, attach or link to the collated raw notes.

That's it. That's all you need to do for the meeting summary. It's simple really. *But wait!* you object, *Shouldn't it be more complicated than that?* Perhaps. But improving upon the summary is something for the team to do in the CA summary meeting. For now, your job is done.

CUSTOMER ALIGNMENT SUMMARY MEETING

The customer alignment summary meeting should be held within two business days of the CA meeting. The host brings the collated notes he's collected from all the scribes, plus the summary document he's prepared.

The purpose of the summary meeting isn't to discuss what you're going to do with the information you learned. No. It's to come to agreement on what was heard. People can sit in the same meeting and hear different things. That can cause problems later when one person says XYZ Corp wants low power at all costs and another person says XYZ Corp wants high performance at all costs. Don't wait until a planning meeting to hash this stuff out. Hash it out in the summary meeting.

Here are topics to discuss:

Review main takeaways from the customer alignment meeting. Review what was heard during the wrap-up portion. Come to agreement on what this discussion revealed about what the customer cares about.

Identify the top three to five goals that the customer identified. Review each of the customer's answers to the question "What would happen if you did nothing to make progress toward this goal?" Note whether they are imperative goals or more nice-to-have goals.

Identify the top three to five challenges the customer will be facing. If anyone asked the customer "What would happen if you did nothing to address this obstacle?" review how the customer answered that question. That will tell you a lot about the importance of the issue.

Map the customer to a schema. Schemas are patterns common to all members of a class. Your schema classes could be market segments. For example, we had automotive, industrial, wireline, wireless, data center, consumer, and so on. Discuss how customer XYZ Corp is similar to other customers within their market space. You may have subschemas as well.

After you've mapped the customer to a preexisting schema, now comes the fun part. It's a treasure hunt. **Find disconfirming facts.** Look through the notes and summary document and identify comments that run against the tide of what other customers within their schema care about. Discuss these disconfirming factors. Answer these questions:

- Is the disconfirming fact relevant to your products?

- Does the disconfirming fact challenge conventional wisdom within your company?

- Can the disconfirming fact be explained away by some external factor?

- Might the disconfirming fact be indicative of a new trend that you should monitor?

Discuss the answers to all these questions and decide what it means. Be fearless and get accustomed to various customers having different goals and challenges.

Compare what you heard with other customers from this company. Say you just met with Joe from XYZ Corp. Three months ago, you met with Diane and Tanner from XYZ Corp. Six months ago, you met with their colleague Rajiv. Tease out messages that are consistent between all the customer's representatives and identify inconsistencies. People from the same company rarely agree on everything. By reviewing the agreements and the inconsistencies, you can get a better idea of the full story. This practice has the added benefit of combating group attribution error, whereby people assume the opinions of a single person represent those of an entire group. Discuss the various stories and you'll learn a more accurate, if more nuanced, picture of what's going on.

Identify stakeholders within your organization who should be made aware of what was learned in this customer alignment meeting. These are people who would be able to do their jobs better if they had access to the meeting notes. If it's a matter of informing a standard set of stakeholders that the summary is complete and where they can access it, the host can handle that. However, if there was some specific technology discussion that a specific group needs to be made aware of, now is the time to assign a specific attendee, usually a subject matter expert or presenter, to take that information to the people who need to know about it.

This step is tricky. Why? Because we don't all know what everyone else in the company is interested in or what they're working on. For example, an engineer in operations may be analyzing the way customers use particular devices. I don't even know that person exists, and he doesn't know about the customer alignment program. Yet we might have discussed his pet topic with the customer. Use the summary meeting to find out if any attendees know these sorts of people.

Next, make sure that all the information gets posted to a centrally accessible location. That way, if at some point the operations engineer is made aware of the CA program, he can search the database or ask someone with access privileges to search it.

If your IT infrastructure allows tagging of portions of notes, take the time to tag the notes with metadata. With search tags—sort of like SEO keywords or Twitter hashtags—search functions improve.

As already mentioned, IT implementation is beyond the scope of this book. What I'd like you to keep in mind is that you may not identify all the stakeholders on your own when you're sitting at your desk. Use the mind-share available to you in the summary meeting to identify all possible stakeholders and come up with a plan to get the summary and the meeting notes or a portion of the meeting notes to every stakeholder who is identified. Assign these as action items. Barring that, make sure the information is put in a central, searchable location (with appropriate security mechanisms in place).

Last, keep in mind that customer information can be abused. People with access to the database have the power to cherry-pick information to make a case for plans they think make sense. This is something you'll need to risk. I would recommend that when you give people access to the customer notes database, you tell them it's their responsibility to search for *disconfirming* as well as *confirmational* data points. That will only go so far, however. The best thing you can do is create a culture where a lot of people attend a lot of CA meetings *and* follow-up meetings. This army of people, aligned with customers, will be your defense against cherry-picking data to make disingenuous cases for product development.

Review action items. Yes, this is boring. Lucky you! It's optional. If your colleagues can be trusted to close out their own action items, then you don't have to run through them all. The exception would be if there are any action items that merit discussing in order to better understand what was learned in the customer alignment meeting.

When I ran CA meetings, I made it clear that I expected people to follow up with customers and the sales team directly. I asked them to copy the host or meeting organizer on all their communications with the customer. I intentionally did not track action items because I didn't want to take on that role. I didn't want people relying on me to remind them to do the work that they signed up for.

This portion of the summary meeting—the review of action items—is about making sure that each action item owner understands that it's up to him or her to close it out. No one is going to babysit them, and everyone expects them to do what they said they would in a timely manner.

Discuss open questions. Not every question gets answered in a customer alignment meeting, and oftentimes the customer's story begets new questions, as does the summary meeting discussion. If the team decides there are any outstanding questions of high importance, then the host can add the specific question to the thank-you e-mail he'll be sending to the customers. Use your best judgment here. Think about the rapport you had with the customer. If it was warm and open and forthright, then send a question or two with the e-mail. However, if the rapport was stiff and formal, you may want to work with the sales team to come up with a strategy for getting these follow-up questions answered. That said, even if the rapport was friendly, don't send too many questions by e-mail. Limit yourself to one or two. These customers aren't employed by your company. Don't ask too much of them. They already took hours out of their busy schedules to talk with you. Don't hog their time any more than you already have.

Review the team's aligning skills. Call out people who demonstrated skillful active listening techniques such as crafting open-ended questions, being comfortable with silence, or using restatement to great effect. If anyone dropped an effective Cunningham bomb, give them a round of applause. They are heroes.

Give thanks to the people who submitted their notes on time and point out a set of notes that was particularly clear, verbatim, and clean to read. Show it as an example of best practices. When you call out the behavior you want to see, you're more likely to see more of that behavior in the future. Don't skip this step.

Show everyone where they can access all the documents associated with this and other customer alignment meetings. Make sure they understand how to access, search, and interact with the system. If you are able to implement an excellent IT system, you still need to make sure that people are aware of it and know how to use it. This is an ideal time to remind them, when they're sated with information they've been starving for: high-quality insights into what customers are trying to do and what problems customers are trying to solve. Show them the path toward getting more such information in the future by pointing out how to access the data effectively.

FINAL FOLLOW-UP

After the customer alignment summary meeting, there are still a few loose ends to tie up.

Send verbatim notes to the customers.

As soon as you've received notes from all the scribes, collate them into a single document. Double-check that they are readable and that they only contain verbatim quotes from the customer. Remove any side-margin commentary or interpretations.

Adjust the notes as needed based on the CA summary discussion. For example, if someone has already closed on an action item, you can mention that fact in the relevant portion of the notes.

Then, along with a heartfelt thank-you in the body of the e-mail, send off the notes to the customer. In the thank-you note, ask the customer to review the notes from the meeting and reply with any corrections for things that were misheard or with additional comments that the team failed to capture. Cite the target date for the next meeting and say you're looking forward to meeting again. Once more, thank them for their time.

Enter a reminder for the next meeting in your calendar.

Does the customer want to meet in eighteen months? Then set an appointment with the sales team for sixteen months from now. On that call, you can get started planning the next customer alignment meeting.

Distribute the customer alignment meeting summary to internal stakeholders.

If you've set up an elegant IT infrastructure, then internal stakeholders should be notified as soon as the customer alignment meeting summary is posted to the system. If your IT infrastructure is less than awesome, then manually make sure all relevant internal stakeholders are notified about what you learned in the meeting. Luckily, you identified them in the summary meeting.

That's it for final follow-up.

That's all? Well, that's it for now. I would suggest you store the raw information and summary documents in such a way that they are easy to access in the future. Consider formally presenting "What We've Heard from CA Meetings Lately" every six months or so to a mixed crowd of internal stakeholders. It's not easy to do because customers vary widely in their goals and challenges. That's all the more reason to present this information. It keeps people from adopting simplistic schemas that make them blind to emerging trends or issues. It helps people maintain a flexible mind-set that is capable of assimilating new information. Consider inviting people responsible for various end markets to present the latest that's been learned in their markets. Make sure they have access to all the notes and understandings of the most recent CA meetings. I'll leave it to you to collate information from all your alignment meetings. Keep an open mind and see what stories emerge. Present these to people who develop, influence, and plan your products.

CHAPTER SIXTEEN

Bringing It All Together

"There is nothing like returning to a place that remains unchanged to find the ways in which you yourself have altered." —Nelson Mandela

CLOSE ALL INFORMATION BLACK HOLES

You know your primary objective in a customer alignment meeting: to discover customer goals and challenges. You know questioning pitfalls to avoid and that assessing customer needs takes more skill and effort than simply asking customers what they want. But if you stop there and fail to continually align with each customer, you risk creating an information black hole.

Consider this question: Why do customers take time out of their busy schedules to meet with you and share their visions of the future? Is it out of the kindness of their hearts? No. They hope to gain something.

Before inviting a customer in for a meeting, first consider what they want to get out of it.

Take a walk in their shoes. Imagine you use a web hosting service called Blue Ops. Now imagine a product planner at Blue Ops invites you to an alignment meeting. In this meeting, the planners listen to your every word and ask thought-provoking questions. You share your vision of an awesome website management dashboard. The Blue Ops employees listen intently and write down every word. They share time-saving tips and challenge your assumptions and make you think. Together, you brainstorm new ideas. You leave, inspired and hopeful.

Two weeks go by; a month; then a year. You hear nothing. You wonder whether you were heard. You upgrade to the new toolset and are disappointed to discover the management dashboard is the same as before. A seed of resentment germinates. Another year passes. The web tools don't change. Resentment grows every time you log on. The bugs remain, and any changes amount to little more than window-dressing. Orange Goods, a competitor of Blue Ops, sends you a compelling offer to switch over to them. You accept.

Now that you're the customer, try answering the question posed above: What did you want to get out of that alignment meeting?

In my experience, the answer boils down to two objectives:

1. The customer wants the company to improve their products in line with the customer's goals.

2. The customer wants to be heard.

In our example, the customer (you) got neither outcome from Blue Ops. While you may not have expected immediate action, the ensuing radio silence made it impossible to know whether you were heard. The lack of product improvements over time indicated that if you were heard, you were subsequently ignored. You spilled your heart and got nothing in return. Blue Ops, a company you'd previously admired, created an information black hole, and you rightfully moved on.

A professional company can and should do better. If you want to be part of an alignment program, don't even think about inviting a customer to align until everyone understands the preparation work and postmeeting procedures to be carried out.

Here are five black-hole busters. If followed, these should meet the minimum needs and expectations of customers who attend customer alignment meetings, all while minimizing the amount of work on your end.

1. During the first meeting, agree on when to meet next.

2. Send a copy of the notes to the customer within a few days (one week maximum).

3. Close every action item in a timely manner.

4. Incorporate the customer's care-abouts into your product development database.

5. When you meet again, present slides that show "What We Heard Last Time," plus updates on developments.

Carry out these five steps and your customers will at the very least feel heard. These steps may seem sparse and that's by design. It's unrealistic to expect the team to maintain monthly contact with every customer. But that shouldn't stop you from aligning with them. Be sure you record what they said, send them a copy, close action items, use their information in your planning activities, and provide an update the next time you meet.

Getting all five activities done takes discipline from the troops and leadership from those responsible for aligning with customers. These five policy expectations must be explicitly stated and carried out as standard operating procedures. Otherwise, as obvious as they are, they won't happen.

Here are some tips for each of the above points to help set expectations and get buy-in.

1. During the wrap-up sessions of the customer alignment meeting, **ask the customer when she'd like to meet next.** It could be anywhere from six months to two years. As noted previously, I recommend meeting once or twice per development cycle. Immediately after the CA meeting, enter this future date into the calendar, with a reminder to confirm with the customer, adjust, and take care of other details two months before the subsequent meeting.

2. **Assign notetakers or scribes** during each segment of the meeting. Make sure someone is always taking verbatim notes that reflect what the customer says. Pull the notes together, proofread them, and send a thank-you e-mail, along with the notes and action items, directly to the customer. You can include the status of actions if you want, but don't let outstanding action items stop you from sending the notes. Sending the notes within a few days is a must!

3. **Set expectations in the internal premeeting** that all attendees are expected to record and follow up on their own action items. Ask the salespeople to record all action items in the meeting and track their closure as a backup precaution.

4. How to **incorporate customer comments** into your product development apparatus is beyond the scope of this book, let alone this bullet point. For now, simply make sure to write up the notes, close action items, and place the notes in a centralized and searchable repository immediately.

5. Last, **have a post-mortem meeting** where the team discusses and agrees upon what was heard. It's common for people to attend the same meeting and take away different messages. The only way to clear up misunderstandings is to talk with one another. It can't be left to chance. Schedule a postmeeting and have that discussion. Follow up with the customer to clarify points of misunderstanding if you feel that's necessary. Then communicate what was heard to internal stakeholders.

6. When the customer returns, start the meeting by **presenting what he told you last time** and report relevant developments since that last meeting.

Long story short: policies must be established, communicated, and followed. Everyone is on a team, and everyone needs to know that aligning with customers goes way beyond simply attending meetings. Follow these rules, and customers will want to continue aligning. Ignore them, and customers will feel they are talking into a black hole. Good luck getting them to meet again!

BEWARE GROUP ATTRIBUTION ERROR

On occasion, you might talk with a customer who, while convincing, turns out to be wrong. Maybe he doesn't really speak for his company or he misunderstands his own product. If you were then to extrapolate that one person's story as being representative of the entire company that employs him or, worse, of an entire end market, you'd be making a grievous mistake.

Indeed, even if you talk to a customer who seems to be intimately familiar with the dynamics of her company's product development, you run the risk of missing critical perspectives if you choose to talk only with that one person. To make sure you get the whole story, it's prudent to talk with others in that customer's company and/or end market as well. Talk to them even if simply to confirm what you've heard.

Group attribution error is the tendency to believe that specific characteristics or behaviors of an individual are reflective of a larger group.

Early in my career, I made such a group attribution error. It nearly cost me my reputation, and it could have negatively impacted my career.

I'd had a conversation with a customer who made televisions and various kinds of displays. This customer asked for a product from us with specific features for his particular application. I knew we were capable of building what he asked for. So far, so good. The customer then claimed that he would ship millions of units a year. The revenue potential was overwhelming.

This particular customer was a niche player in the larger market. Having some idea of who the main players were, I extrapolated and estimated our potential revenue into the tens of millions. Dollar signs flashed in my retinas.

I barged into my boss's office like an eager little beaver and reported the news. He laughed and quickly brought me back to reality. He explained that the customer would never go to full production with our flexible and relatively expensive devices. As soon as cheap mass-market and specialized devices became available, the customer would replace us. Apparently, this was common knowledge in the industry. To be sure, in subsequent meetings I heard other TV customers readily admit that they would cease using our products as soon as cheaper devices were introduced.

Looking back, it's clear I made two rookie mistakes. First, I failed to ask questions to understand the use model from the customer's perspective. I failed to determine how long the customer would use our devices, what their trade-offs were, how important cost reductions would be, or what they truly needed in order to meet their objectives. Second, and perhaps more egregious, I assumed this customer's comments represented an entire market.

Luckily for me, my boss pointed out my error privately before I could make an idiot of myself in front of a wider audience. Looking back, knowing what I know now, I might have lost a lot of credibility with my colleagues had I presented that case. That day, I gained a healthy respect for group attribution error, and for my boss.

To avoid group attribution error, you must acknowledge that a single customer opinion does not represent the summation of all opinions held within that customer's company, not to mention an overall end market.

Deliberately talk to many customers. Invite two or three people from a single customer division to a customer alignment meeting. Sometimes they'll hash out their disagreements in the meeting. That can be illuminating. Another strategy is to hold multiple CA meetings with different people from a single company.

Do your homework, and go out of your way to talk to customers who are well respected within their fields. Even for these paragons of illuminating insights, bear in mind that they don't necessarily represent the entirety of their end markets. You still need to talk with other people. Definitely give these people's opinions the weight they deserve. But listen to others as well.

Last, participate in follow-up meetings. This is where the team discusses inconsistencies between various customers from a single company, or from the wider industry. It's in these meetings where schemas are updated and the team is best able to tease out fact from fiction.

Teams that are aware of group attribution error, and that discuss how various customer stories compare, build up an immunity to bad information from a single source. If you make a habit of talking with multiple people in an industry, you'll eventually suss out misinformation. If you don't, you might jump to wrongheaded conclusions and build products that don't sell.

ALIGN WITH MANY OR NONE AT ALL

In previous chapters, schemas got a bad rap, as we learned they could keep us blind to considering new information. They filter episodic memory, thereby reinforcing existing beliefs. But they can be useful too.

Schemas help us calmly take in the torrent of data we encounter every second. Without them, we'd be overwhelmed. They are a way to get a handle on large chunks of information. They enable us to communicate complex concepts quickly.

Schemas can manifest as what you might recognize as gut instinct. This happens when our brain shortcuts to an answer before we have a chance to cognitively analyze a situation. This can be life-saving or lucrative if one's schemas are correct. Schemas are central components to how we think. They're unavoidable. So it's up to us to make sure they are as true to reality as possible. The first step is to develop the tools to combat confirmation bias and group attribution error. The second step is to increase the data set that schemas derive from. In short, talk to more customers.

In my experience, colleagues who talked with only two or three customers a year possessed dangerously narrow and distorted customer schemas. In internal planning meetings, they tended to think they knew what customers wanted, but really they only knew what one or two customers wanted. And they were confident. I now understand that I was witnessing the Dunning-Kruger effect, a phenomenon where people with less knowledge tend to be more confident than people with more knowledge in a given subject.

In these meetings, it seemed that rather than picking up on underlying patterns, these onesie-twosie meeting attendees had the potential to delay developments or throw plans off track. By citing a real customer who didn't want a feature we were planning for, they would make a powerful case for delaying development of that feature. If decision makers didn't know the dynamics of the wider markets, they could be duped into agreeing to the delays.

This wasn't simply an oversight. Some people I've worked with went out of their way to choose just one customer to align with. Some would argue that talking to fewer customers was the best strategy. A single clear message from one well-chosen customer would allow the team to avoid the cross talk, noise, and uncertainty that came with speaking to multiple customer voices.

They had a point. The ambiguity of multiple conflicting voices could lead to confusion, second-guessing, and delays. However, I contend that too narrow a focus on just one customer can lead to trouble. The assumption that one customer represents an entire end market, in my experience, is rarely true. The planners who tended to call the market right were the people who talked to as many customers as possible, not fewer. They had the ability to listen to one customer at a time with full attention and then incorporate that new information into their schemas in an appropriate proportion. It's hard work. But it's the only way, as far as I can tell, of developing schemas that reflect reality.

So what's the right number of customers to talk to? Depending on your industry, a minimum should be fifteen within a year, but I'd recommend twenty to thirty. These numbers come from a couple decades of personal experience, but the concept is readily explained by drawing parallels with modern portfolio theory in the world of stock investing.

Modern portfolio theory is based on the premise that increasing the number of low-correlated stocks within a portfolio lowers the risk of the portfolio as a whole. Risk drops significantly as you move from holding one stock to holding two. It continues to drop markedly as you increase from three to four, on up to about fifteen. After fifteen stocks are in your portfolio, risk continues to drop but not as dramatically. Many investment advisers agree that a portfolio with thirty low-correlated stocks is ideal for minimizing risk.

The numbers seem to be similar with a portfolio of customers with whom goals and challenges have been uncovered. The more customers whose unbiased and complete stories are understood, the greater the chance that one's schema is going to represent the market.

If your products or services sell into multiple end markets, you might want to talk to fifteen to thirty customers within each end market. At the very least, make sure that employees who are responsible for each of those end markets talk to that many customers.

During the first seven or so customer visits, one's view of the customer perspective is rapidly forming. People are still open-minded, searching for patterns and hearing new viewpoints.

At somewhere around fifteen customer interviews, people have glimpsed some patterns and repetitions. Their schema is taking shape. That's great. But a word of caution: This is a dangerous time. They're like teenagers who think they know it all, which makes them particularly prone to confirmation bias. At this point, especially, make sure that members of the aligning team continue to seek out discordant information that doesn't jibe. Have them ask seemingly stupid questions, make sure they take verbatim notes, and confirm they're using active listening questions and active listening after questions in customer uncovering sessions. Talk about it! Discuss the difference between pursuing a specific outcome based on hunches and seeking truths no matter where they may lead.

A team member who has met with more than thirty customers tends to understand that customers can be all over the map in terms of goals and objectives. It's at this point that some of the more fundamental customer attributes come through.

For example, it was after talking in-depth with at least about thirty customers when a conventional wisdom truly sunk in. I'd heard that our customers cared about Time to Market (TTM). Our products enabled customers to get to market with new technologies faster than with alternatives. I remember talking with a customer a few years ago into my career in product planning, when I came to truly appreciate the importance and primacy of this "need" for TTM. Their whole existence hinged on getting to market fast. It was as if my understanding of this "customer need" transitioned from academic hand-waving into a profound visceral truth.

After that realization, I strove to find instances where time to market was not a concern for customers. I rarely found such examples. Thus, this became one of the foundational elements of my overall customer schema. This understanding made its way into trade-off discussion meetings. In the background, I would think about how various product trade-offs would affect time to market. It made me better at my job. With the principle of time to market as a part of my customer schema, I was positioned to better represent the true motivations of customers in internal planning meetings.

Time to market is just one example that tended to apply to all our customers. There were other schema elements I adopted that varied from end market to end market. The point is you can't be sure you've developed accurate customer schemas if you only talk to a few customers. You need to talk to dozens.

If the team firmly establishes habits such as retaining genuinely curious mind-sets, asking ALQ/ALAQs, and writing verbatim notes, aligning with customers gets easier. The team will continue to be on the lookout for new information, whether it jibes with their schemas or not. They'll write verbatim notes, so they have a true record of what the customer actually said versus a bullet-point list of fragmented comments they wanted to hear.

Stay on the lookout for disconfirming or oddball comments. When such triggers trip, double down on uncovering what's really going on. Meet with dozens of customers, and you'll discover insights that really matter.

CHAPTER SEVENTEEN

Common Meeting Traps and How to Avoid Them

"What is this? Amateur hour?"
—Ron Burgundy, *Anchorman: The Legend of Ron Burgundy*

A STORY OF WRONG TURNS AND BAD ASSUMPTIONS

IN CUSTOMER MEETINGS, I've notably witnessed colleagues fail to learn what customers needed or wanted. I've seen coworkers write down requirements that were dead wrong.

Even the most socially or technically aware individuals can get tripped up. The risk isn't limited to burning a relationship. The real risk is walking away with incorrect information. Here's an example.

Once upon a time, before undergoing training, my colleagues and I nearly walked away from a customer alignment meeting thinking the customer required a costly feature, when in reality he did not. We had asked one seemingly simple question and that question elicited information that was dead wrong. Here is the story. (Details have been changed to avoid disclosing proprietary information, names have been changed to protect the guilty, and uBit is a fictional technology.)

Carl, a customer and highly respected system architect from a midsize company, had presented his road map. My coworker began his presentation. Our intention was to validate product plans and to gather further inputs to inform outstanding decisions. One such intensely debated decision was whether to remove support for a legacy technology, uBit. Most of us were in favor of cutting uBit support from the product.

Carl hadn't expressed a need for uBit during his two-hour-long road map presentation. Rather than assuming uBit to be a "don't care," someone from my team rightly asked Carl about it. "Do you need uBit?"

Carl sat bolt upright and replied, "Definitely!" His response surprised me. My colleagues immediately took defensive postures and began exploring whether other solutions would be acceptable to him. By brainstorming alternatives, they signaled reluctance to support uBit. Carl grew angry, and the meeting took a bad turn.

While everyone was bickering, Carl glowered, turned bright red, and stared at his folded hands. He'd disconnected from the conversation. At long last, someone asked, "Carl, what capabilities will you gain in your next-generation product by using uBit?"

Normal coloring returned to his face and he replied, "Well, uBit allows us to connect to a legacy processor. We use that processor for board management and system control."

Someone then asked, "What else is the microprocessor used for?"

He replied, "Just board management and system control. In fact, the only reason we need uBit is to talk to that processor."

He grew quiet and then admitted, "Actually, we have to drop that processor. We received an end-of-life notice from the manufacturer and need to look for alternatives."

He added, "You know, for our next project, I don't think we need uBit at all."

WHAT?!@#$%?

We recorded Carl's comments and moved on. At the end of the meeting, we even helped brainstorm ways Carl could solve his end-of-life issue. That was a close shave!

What happened? What had gone wrong? We'd asked, "Do you need uBit?" It's a deceptively simple sentence. It's just four words, and it's straightforward. Yet this question exemplifies what *not* to ask.

Here's a diagnosis of some of the traps we fell into in this meeting, followed by even more traps to be aware of. There are many.

GETTING STUCK IN TODAY

When Carl hears "Do you need uBit?" he answers in consideration of his current product. The questioning team, on the other hand, really wants to know about future requirements. By asking a question in the present tense, the two sides talk in different time frames. The uncovering team believes Carl has a strong requirement for uBit in the future, but his requirement has to do with his current product—because the question was framed using the present tense.

The remedy is to ask about the future. Simply be clear about the time frame. A better question would have been "Will you need uBit in new designs on the drawing board now, for implementation over the next few years?" This is better in that it clearly asks Carl to think about his future products. However, this is still suboptimal.

ASKING YES/NO QUESTIONS

Carl answered the uBit question in one word. He didn't explain why he needed uBit or in what configuration. Why should he have explained further? He was asked a yes/no question, after all. As we've discussed, problems with yes/no questions are many. For one, the presumption is that there are only two possible answers. Second, they fail to prompt an explanation. Third, yes/no questions fail to get at *why*.

Instead of asking yes/no questions, ask open-ended questions. If your question starts with *Do* or *Will*, you are probably asking a yes/no question. Instead, start your question with *What*, *Which*, or *Why*. A better question would have been "What capabilities will you gain in your next-generation product by implementing uBit?" This one is not only open-ended but framed in the future as well. Win, win.

FAILING TO ASK WHY

Yes/no questions are unskillful but can be resolved by simply following up with "Why?" However, in our example, the team didn't try to understand why Carl needed uBit. Instead, they jumped into brainstorming alternative solutions rather than doubling down on learning *why* he needed uBit.

The team led Carl down a path of investigating solutions that would conform to our road map. This was off-putting, to say the least. It would have been far better to focus on what Carl was trying to achieve instead. If we had asked a future-focused open-ended question that asked Why?, we would have learned all we needed. For example, a better question might have been "What design goals are driving you to use uBit in your next-generation products?"

DROPPING DOWN THE RABBIT HOLE

The rabbit hole is a trap that a colleague of mine used to call a "rat's nest." I'm not really sure what a rat's nest looks like, so I'm going with rabbit hole. In truth, it's how friendly conversation often progresses, but it's not ideal for a customer alignment meeting.

Imagine that topic A is being discussed. One person comments and, in doing so, broaches topic B. Another person elaborates on topic B with gusto, whether or not everyone is done discussing topic A. Now the discussion is on B, and the team fails to return to topic A. They move on to topic C and then D.

A rabbit hole is when the conversation dives into parenthetical territory before the original question has been answered. Diving into rabbit holes comes naturally and can be interesting. But it's undisciplined behavior and may leave you holding only superficial answers, preventing you from obtaining substantial and useful answers.

In chapters seven and eight on the art of questioning, I explained how to ask open-ended questions and how to follow up with ones that elicit more answers to the same topic. Sticking with the topic takes discipline and conscious intent. If there's even one person who has not learned how to ask active listening questions, you are likely to get diverted down an orthogonal rabbit hole. All it takes is for the customer to answer with a comment that piques an attendee's curiosity. And bam! Off topic. Make sure everyone on your team has read this book or taken training based on these concepts. Otherwise you risk receiving incomplete and superficial answers to your questions.

BAILING OUT THE CUSTOMER

Remember when you were the legal vice president in "winging it" scenarios of chapter six? Someone on your team asked the customer about future challenges. The customer squirmed silently, so you bailed him out by providing a multiple-choice list of possible answers.

Bad move! By bailing out the customer, you caused two problems.

One, you disrupted the customer's thinking. When a customer hears a question and then goes quiet, he's contemplating his answer. That's golden! You want him reaching deep for the real answer. If you interrupt him with a bailout, you've just sealed off the mine to customer gold—precisely the information that everyone in the meeting is there to hear.

Two, by offering a menu of options to choose from, you narrow his answer set and lead him to responses that come from your own bias. When you bail out the customer with a list of options, you taint the sample set. At that point, if he agrees to any of your offered answers, you can't fully trust the data.

Remember: when you bail out the customer, you're doing no one any favors. Not only are you cutting off his train of thought, but you're leading the witness. You're tainting the evidence. You don't want to be an evidence tainter. Do you?

SETTING THE CUSTOMER STRAIGHT

Imagine the customer is clearly misinformed. For example, she's saying that as semiconductor geometries shrink, she's looking forward to benefiting from lower power.

Ha! you think. You know that power doesn't necessarily drop with transistor gate length. Indeed, when the gate decreases in size, current leakage through the dielectric increases. That means you burn more power. Extra circuitry must be used to fully shut off the gate. That, in effect, increases the geometric size of the transistor.

As a result, the actual die size must increase in order to prevent leakage power from dominating.

If you were in a meeting with a colleague, you could set him straight and explain all the factors that go into total power as gate lengths decrease. You could sketch it out on the whiteboard for hours if he wanted to get into the topic deeply. In other kinds of meetings, discussing changes in dynamic and static power as gate size varies might be perfectly fine. But this is a customer meeting. Now is not the time to set the customer straight. For one thing, you'd be derailing the meeting down a rabbit hole. For another, the details of implementation of your product are likely not within the areas of the customer's expertise. Even if he knows his semiconductor physics backward and forward, you are not in the meeting to discuss your own engineering trade-offs.

So what do you do? You double down on uncovering, that's what. You could ask, "What specifically is driving your need for lower dynamic power?" Follow up with questions like "What else?" or "Anything else?" After you've caught all the answers to the question about dynamic power, then you ask, "What specific factors or objectives are driving your need for lower static power? What else? Any other factors driving your need for low static power?" Then you can ask about what's driving the need for smaller geometries.

Note that you didn't ask, "What's your dynamic/static power goal?" Sure, you might get a quantitative answer, but you won't know the reason behind it. Good luck using that data point in a planning meeting when someone with a lot of influence is trying to relax power goals. If you know the specific power requirements of this customer, it may be useful, but not nearly as powerful as being able to explain the reasons and urgency for the power goals. The best way to get to those answers is to ask active listening questions.

Sure, you can follow up with a specific clarifying question, such as "What specifically are your static and dynamic power budgets?" But don't start there. And you'll probably find that the customer volunteers this information anyway as he answers your open-ended future-focused active listening question.

But wait, you say. *What if power was brought up as an answer to another open-ended question, and the customer hadn't yet said they were done giving answers to that other question?*

Good catch! What you do is write down your questions and wait until the customer says he's done answering the original question. Then you ask the host or the customer, depending on the dynamics of the meeting, whether you can ask a follow-up question to one of the customer's answers.

ASKING QUESTIONS "OUT OF CURIOSITY"

While it's true that genuine curiosity should drive questions asked in a customer alignment meeting, questions that start with "I'm just curious" or "Out of curiosity" come off badly. They feel like afterthoughts, as if the questioner doesn't really care what the answer is, or is somehow failing to value the customer's time.

I've asked colleagues why they start questions this way. Typically, they do it without thinking. But when they consider what's really going on, they usually say it's for one of two reasons.

One, it's an equivocation. It's an effort to soften the punch of a question, to avoid putting the customer on the spot. It's to give the customer an out if they can't answer or don't want to answer. As if the question isn't important.

Here's the thing: The people who are invited to customer alignment meetings typically know their subjects. Also, they're adults. If they're asked for information they'd rather not divulge or they simply don't know, they can say as much. If you began the meeting by connecting appropriately with the customers and listening to them first, then these direct questions should be fine.

The second reason one might start a question with "I'm just curious" or "Out of curiosity" is that it's born of trivial curiosity. Save such questions for break time. Don't derail the meeting because you're mildly curious about something that's off topic.

Here's a suggestion: If you feel yourself starting a question with "Out of curiosity," take a moment to consider your question. Think about why you are prepending this phrase. If it's to avoid putting the customer on the spot, then put that out of your mind. Rephrase the question to conform to active listening guidelines, wait for the appropriate time, then ask with confidence. It's great to ask such questions from a place of ardent curiosity where you're trying to understand the customer's situation. Just kill the equivocal "Out of curiosity" portion. If, on the other hand, you want more information about some triviality, then save the question for break time over lunch, or over dinner or never.

PING-PONG QUESTIONING

Remember the scenario where you were the customer and Bob and Tom were interrogating you about your financial situation? How annoying was that? Bob would ask one selfish question and before you could really answer, Tom would jump in with questions about a totally different topic.

Bob and Tom were hungry for customer data within their own areas of interest but held no regard for what you, as the customer, cared about. The back-and-forth questioning was not only fatiguing, but the questions didn't even really apply to your situation. Bob and Tom behaved selfishly, and it left you, the customer, feeling annoyed.

This Ping-Pong questioning seems absurd, but it happens way more often than I would have predicted. Invite two people who haven't gone through customer alignment training, and I guarantee that if they get it in their minds that it's a free-for-all question-and-answer session, you'll find yourself in the middle of a Ping-Pong match. It isn't pretty.

RAPID-FIRE QUESTIONING

The uncovering team made up of Bob and Tom fell into another common trap. Like a breathless toddler, Tom rapid-fired off multiple questions as if he only had that one minute to squeeze all his questions in.

Now, his questions may have been legitimate. However, by firing them off all at once, he had little chance of receiving answers to *all* the questions. Indeed, in our example, you, the customer, responded only to the last question.

Don't be a three-year-old in a customer alignment meeting. Act like a conscientious adult and ask one well-crafted question at a time. If you write down your questions prior to uttering them, you'll find that you get higher-quality and more complete answers than if you rapid-fire multiple questions off at once.

LOADED QUESTIONS

People come to customer alignment meetings with all kinds of agendas. Often they're under pressure to make trade-off decisions about a product being developed. Include feature A or keep it in for backward compatibility? Add feature B, or scrap it? Usually, people faced with these decisions already have an idea of what the right answer should be. If so, they may ask loaded questions. Whether intentional or not, loaded questions steer customers toward answers the questioner wants to hear. This is confirmation bias at work.

Loaded questions are often closed-ended or multiple-choice. Both types narrow the universe of possible answers. Remember our legal vice president of engineering who bailed out the customer with his preconceived ideas of what the customer thought? By definition, these were answers the vice president already believed were true. By stating them, he led the customer toward his own biased answers, even if he was unaware of this.

Worse yet, I've seen people come into meetings determined to trick the customer into giving specific answers. They were like single-minded prosecutors, going after convictions, no matter the facts. In pursuit of specific answers, the truth became irrelevant.

For example, one colleague I worked with already had decided we needed to improve the speed of a particular circuit. For our purposes here, we'll call it "blip." He'd encountered tremendous pushback from the engineering department, which didn't see why the existing circuitry was inadequate. He was eager to find customer data points to support his recommendation to improve blip. At a customer alignment meeting, the first question he asked was "Do you want a faster blip circuit?"

Well, that's a loaded question. What's the customer going to say? "No"? In this case, and to his credit, the customer actually said he wasn't sure how to answer. So my colleague led him further down the path. He said, "Other customers have told us that if the blip circuit increases to x speed, they'll be able to operate more reliably."

What do you think the customer is going to say to that? Of course he said, "That sounds good. Sure, I would like that."

My colleague then recorded this customer as being someone who needs blip at x speed. My friend from engineering witnessed this as well. He was fuming. Our colleague was behaving like William J. Casey, as we discussed in chapter eleven on "Combating Confirmation Bias." Fortunately for us, we were able to successfully argue against counting that customer as a data point. And my colleague lost all credibility in our department and among the engineering department. I tried to coach him to ask open-minded questions. But he couldn't see what he'd done wrong. Soon after that incident, he transitioned to working for another company.

By asking loaded questions, my colleague turned a customer from not caring in the least bit about the blip circuitry into someone who, according to him, vehemently needed blip to run at x speed. His actions in that meeting led to a gathering of information we couldn't use because he'd led the witness to the answer he wanted to hear. This was blatant confirmation bias. Stick to active listening questions and you'll avoid this.

SIGN ALL NONDISCLOSURE AGREEMENTS BEFORE THE CUSTOMER ALIGNMENT MEETING

For us, a standard nondisclosure agreement (NDA) was sufficient to protect us and our customers. In a customer alignment meeting, it's important to be able to share road maps. An NDA must be in place before anyone shares such sensitive information. My recommendation is to require that NDAs be signed before any meeting is held.

SO MANY TRAPS!

There's a lot that can go wrong, but don't worry. If you simply follow the active listening question guidelines and write down what you hear, you're most of the way there. Be gentle with yourself if you mess up. When we're caught up in a conversation, it can be easy to slip into old habits. That's why training and practice are so important. Spend a few minutes before your customer alignment meeting and write down your ALQs. Similarly, during the meeting, if you think of a question to ask, write it down, double-check that it's an ALQ, and wait until an appropriate time to ask it. Formulate the questions with care and you'll increase the likelihood of aligning skillfully.

At this point, it may be worth rereading the section titled "The Aligning Team's Goals" in chapter four. Many of these "gotchas" are covered there as well.

A final thought: Do you remember the story of Detective Bruch of the Virginia Beach Police in chapter nine? It struck me that the detectives in his department seemed more interested in extracting confessions than they were in seeking out the truth. Between confirmation bias, following a selfish agenda, and asking poorly crafted questions, we can easily slip into that line of thinking where we believe our objective is to get the customer to tell us what we want to hear. It's your job to remember that your goal is to seek out the truth, even if that truth doesn't fit into your belief framework. Use the skills you've learned in this chapter to uncover your customer's goals and challenges and prepare to remain comfortable even when the answers are not what you expected. And then ask, "What else?"

CHAPTER EIGHTEEN

Final Thoughts

"The master has failed more times than the beginner has even tried." —Stephen McCranie

WHAT I'VE DESCRIBED in this book are tips and strategies for aligning with customers, especially in face-to-face meetings, for the purpose of crafting road maps that can result in products that your customers will want. Once these skills become second nature, go out into the world and talk to customers on their turf too. Much can be learned in mini-customer alignment meetings out in the field. Most of the active listening and other techniques discussed in this book work in these traveling scenarios as well.

Aligning with customers is not a one-time event. It takes ongoing, iterative effort. Sometimes it can be frustrating because customer inputs might not address current questions. Or you might find that some customers don't open up as much as you'd like. Persevere. Keep uncovering and keep developing your skills. Continue talking with customers in a spirit of curiosity and genuine interest. For a few minutes or hours, forget what you know and open your mind to seeing the world from your customers' perspectives. The insights will come. Patience and attentiveness are key.

I've described specific techniques to employ and general mindsets to adopt. It's a lot to take in all at once. But it's worth doing. From crafting open-ended questions to using Cunningham's Law to putting on your detective's hat, these tips, taken together, can lead to discovering the clear-eyed reality of what your customers are trying to do, unfettered from the yoke of confirmation bias.

You now understand the importance of planning these interactions properly and following up in such a way as to make aligning a team effort to develop ongoing relationships with customers.

You understand the importance of talking to multiple customers, going wide across an entire market and deep within a single company. We've touched on cultural considerations and on adjustments to be made when encountering extreme personalities. And you know to pay special attention to comments that are contrary to your conventional wisdom.

I've provided detailed tactical advice for running customer alignment meetings. Take these suggestions as a starting point and adjust as needed. Make the process your own. Whatever you do, the end result should be that you have a team of professionals who get together periodically with customers to genuinely attempt to understand the world from their perspectives. Take notes because you'll be discovering information that matters.

Good luck!

Appendix

CUSTOMER PREP LETTER

THIS IS A QUESTIONNAIRE you can use as a template. It's based on a questionnaire I used in my capacity as a product planning manager. Craft your own and send it to your customer two to three weeks before the customer alignment meeting.

Dear [customer],

Please consider the following questions as you prepare for the upcoming customer alignment meeting with ABC Corp. Sending us the answers one week prior to the meeting will help us craft a suitable agenda and will ensure our time together is as useful for you as possible.

Please use questions 1–3 to develop your slide set that you will present at the meeting and send the answer to question 4 back to [the meeting host] as soon as possible, so he/she can customize the agenda and invite the appropriate attendees.

Questions:
1. What are your top goals? Product goals and market goals in the next three to five years?

2. What metrics have you established for measuring these goals?

3. What obstacles over the next five years might get in the way?

4. You have an R&D budget of $500M to develop the next-generation ABC widgets. You are visiting with the widget planners and can call in any of the key technology engineers responsible for developing widgets. What topics will you want to advise them on? What level of technical discussion will you want to get into? Pick up to five topics that are of highest priority and indicate technical depth.

   1=You have some bits of information to convey.

   2=You have detailed advice to give, including underlying problem to be solved.

   3=You request a comprehensive brainstorming discussion with the resident subject matter experts.

Topic	Level of Discussion	Comments
Topic A		
Topic B		
. . .		
Topic Z		

Thank you.

[your name]

To increase the chances of receiving a reply to the questionnaire, the sales team could set up an in-person meeting with the customer to walk them through the questions and to set expectations about the upcoming customer alignment meeting.

Bibliography

Bender, Peter Urs. *Leadership from Within*. Toronto, Ontario: Stoddart, 1997.

Carnegie, Dale. *How to Win Friends and Influence People*. New York: Simon & Schuster, 1936.

Charvet, Shelle Rose. *Words That Change Minds*. Dubuque, Iowa: Kendall/Hunt Publishing Company, 1995, 1997.

Chodron, Pema. *Start Where You Are*. Boulder, Colorado: Shambhala Publications, Inc., 2001.

Don't Talk to the Police (video with Officer Bruch at Regents University). https://youtu.be/6wXkI4t7nuc

Drucker, Peter. *The Practice of Management*. New York: Harper, 1954.

Dweck, Carol S. *Mindset: The New Psychology of Success*. New York: Ballantine Books, 2008.

Gladwell, Malcolm. *Outliers*. New York: Little, Brown and Company, 2008.

Goleman, Daniel. *Emotional Intelligence: Why It Can Matter More Than IQ*. New York: Bantam Books, 1995.

Heath, Chip, and Dan Heath. *Decisive: How to Make Better Choices in Life and Work*. New York: Currency, 2013.

Heath, Chip, and Dan Heath. *Switch: How to Change Things When Change Is Hard*. Waterville, Maine: Thorndike Press, 2011.

Kinzer, Stephen. *The Brothers: John Foster Dulles, Allen Dulles, and Their Secret World War*. First Edition. New York: Time Books/Henry Holt and Company, 2013.

Marsh, Elizabeth J. "Retelling Is Not the Same as Recalling: Implications for Memory," *Sage Journals*, Volume 16, Issue 1, February 1, 2007.

Meyer, Erin. *The Culture Map: Breaking Through the Invisible Boundaries of Global Business*. New York: PublicAffairs, 2014.

Meyer, Erin. "Getting to Si, Ja, Oui, Hai, and Da," *Harvard Business Review*, December 2015.

Rosenberg, Marshall B. *Nonviolent Communication: A Language of Life*. Encinitas, CA: PuddleDancer Press, 2003.

About the Author

LAURA REESE'S eighteen-year career in the semiconductor industry was largely spent at Altera Corporation, which is now a division of Intel Corporation. As a senior manager in the product planning department, she directed the customer advisory board (CAB) program.

She earned a Bachelor of Science in biomedical and electrical engineering with a business minor from the University of Southern California in 1996. In her spare time, she studied finance through Boston University and earned a Certified Financial Planning certificate from the Certified Financial Planner Board of Standards. In 2014, Laura founded a charity for Rohingya refugees in Malaysia called RohingyaFund.org.

She now lives in Verona, Italy, with her family.